Newcastle Ragged
and Industrial
School

Newcastle Ragged
and Industrial
School

WENDY PRAHMS

TEMPUS

Frontispiece: Part of the original purpose-built Ragged School in Newcastle.

First published 2006

Tempus Publishing Limited
The Mill, Brimscombe Port,
Stroud, Gloucestershire, GL5 2QG
www.tempus-publishing.com

British Library Cataloguing in Publication Data.
A catalogue record for this book is available from the British Library.

ISBN 0 7524 4088 8

Typesetting and origination by Tempus Publishing Limited.
Printed in Great Britain.

Contents

Acknowledgements

I should like to thank the staff of the following: Newcastle City Library Local Studies, especially Sarah Mulligan and Pam Wilson; Gateshead Borough Central Library Local Studies; Tyne and Wear Archives.

Particular thanks go to Ray Marshall of the *Newcastle Evening Chronicle* and also to Professor Norman McCord for valuable criticisms and suggestions which I have tried to act upon.

Picture acknowledgements:

Most illustrations are from Newcastle City Libraries' Local Studies collection and are reproduced with their permission. Those on pages 80, 88, and 86 are reproduced courtesy of Gateshead Borough Libraries' Local Studies collection. Those on pages 34, 38, 46-7, 55, and 73 are reproduced courtesy of Tyne and Wear Archives. Those on pages 10 and 69: permission to reproduce applied for to Northumberland Record Office. The following pictures are reproduced courtesy of: Getty Images (p.67); Blackwell Publishing (p.68); Mary Evans Picture Library (p.62); Mrs Dobie of Newcastle (p.51).

I

What Were the Ragged and Industrial Schools?

The establishment in the first half of the nineteenth century of Ragged Schools, Industrial Schools and Reformatories as well as a growing numbers of Refuges for neglected street children signalled a changed political mood, away from the *laissez faire* of the previous century. The change was partly forced upon society by the huge influx of immigrants into all the major cities brought about by early industrialisation. These people were certainly immigrants despite coming from the British Isles and speaking English. Towns and cities had been an attraction for ambitious poor people ever since the Black Death of the fourteenth century broke once and for all the customary tie between a man and his 'parish'. Towns full of people on the make or on the move were nothing new at the turn of the nineteenth century, but the numbers were. Dispossessed Scottish crofters, uncounted numbers of Irish brought in to cut canals and railway routes, rural workers from all over England either made landless by Enclosures Acts or simply, as nowadays, looking for a better life than incessant toil on a patch of dirt, poured into all the big towns, married, or at any rate bred children, and then set the children to work one way or another. Rural children worked as soon as they could walk; why not these children of the streets? There was plenty of demand for child labour in the coalmines, in the new cotton and woollen mills, in shipyards and in every kind of domestic service including chimney sweeping. Many children worked at regular jobs like adults. Some, however, did not.

Heavy drinking was still habitual among men of all classes at the turn of the nineteenth century; in the working classes, among women too. Gin was plentiful and cheap. This led to neglect of the children and often to worse: children were put out on the street in the morning and told not to come back until they had got something: food, money, items of value, anything. How they got it was up to them: they could work or beg or steal. If these wretched children's parents died they were left utterly bereft and forced to live by their wits. Many were taken into workhouses as a welfare measure, but there was no shortage of 'landlords' to take advantage of those who did not want to go; the 'landlords' would house and feed the children and encourage them to continue their 'work' on the streets. Charles Dickens' Fagin is an obvious fictional example. In their defence it must be said that they did at least provide basic care for the children; the trouble was that many of the children grew to accept the life, and this became a huge social problem. Growing numbers of lawless children on the streets of every city made the middle classes feel unsafe.

Women roofers in
Newcastle, 1820s.

There was another motive for setting up institutions for delinquent children: conscience. Until the Enlightenment crime had always been thought of as a permanent burden on society – part of the general sinfulness of man. Now however it became just one more problem to be solved: remove lawless children from their criminal environment before they had become too steeped in it and fond of it, rear them and teach them among law-abiding, hardworking people, and they would grow up good citizens. Revived Christianity, exemplified by Methodism, combined with the Kantian idea of duty to make fortunate people feel they must do something permanent for the poor.

The Newcastle Ragged and Industrial Schools existed from the 1840s to the 1930s. When I first heard of them I was intrigued; like many people I had a hazy idea what a Ragged School was – the name explains itself though I shall explain it at length later – but I had never heard of Industrial Schools. Were they an early version of the secondary technical schools which the 1944 Education Act had promised and which, except for a few token specimens, never saw the light of day? In any case, why were they not as much part of common knowledge as the Mechanics Institutes – another nineteenth-century enterprise – which are famous for having become the nuclei of many redbrick universities? And how had it come about that two schools in Newcastle, a boys' and a girls', had been both Ragged and Industrial? Before looking at the history of these particular schools we will look at what Industrial Schools were.

8

'Industrial' in their title did not mean 'technological'; it just meant 'to do with work'. 'Being industrious' is probably the best modern equivalent. Briefly, the Industrial Schools were founded to give education, food, lodging, and training in the habits of work to convicted children who had not yet served a prison sentence. This interested me because some years ago (2002) a similar proposal was put before Parliament; the idea was to detect young children who were likely to become criminals, and give them special preventative education. Human and Civil Rights groups opposed the idea and as far as I know it was dropped. But in the mid-nineteenth century the idea was embraced and for about eighty years the Industrial Schools trained, educated, fed and cared for such children over the age of six but under twelve on entry. This upper age limit was raised to fourteen by one of the later Industrial Schools Acts (1884).

Most children were sent on a magistrate's order, having been found guilty of a first criminal offence punishable by imprisonment. Until the Juvenile Offenders Act of 1847 child lawbreakers over seven years of age had been subject to the same penalties as adults, in theory at least. However, in the 1830s child criminals deemed too 'weak' or too young to know what they were doing were often sent to one of the charitable Refuges which had been founded by philanthropists. Magistrates had always had discretion to deal with young offenders other than by ordering adult penalties, and, as a further softening of the rigour of the law, a young criminal who was destitute or orphaned could be sent to the workhouse instead of prison; workhouses, though, applied strict tests of 'destitution' and 'parentlessness'. If a magistrate did commit a child to prison it could be as much for the child's sake as for society's: in prison children were at least fed and sheltered.

The 'Refuges' referred to prefigured the Industrial Schools in many ways, as did other charitable institutions of the time. A 'House of Refuge' for girls, established in the mid-eighteenth century near Westminster Bridge, aimed to rescue girls likely to drift into prostitution and teach them some other way to support themselves. Indeed an unofficial designation of 'Industrial School' or 'School of Industry' had been applied in this country to various establishments for at least a century. 'Industrial School' only became precisely defined to indicate one particular kind of school at a meeting of a Government Select Committee on Criminal and Destitute Juveniles in 1852. The idea of such schools was originally continental. Industrial Schools took root earlier in Scotland than in England and were often identical with the 'Refuges' or linked to them.[1] When Industrial Schools began to be established up and down the whole United Kingdom they were used in the same way by the courts as the Refuges were.

The Industrial Schools Act of 1857 standardised the practice and laid down minimum qualifications for a school to be certified for its purpose. Children were committed on the order of a magistrate or two justices and had to stay in the school for a determined number of years, but not, except in special circumstances, beyond the age of fiftteen. Age on entry to such a school was between seven and twelve years (later fourteen); young offenders older than this could be sent to Reformatories, but only if they had already served a prison sentence.[2] This condition limited the scope of the Reformatories from the start and was one reason they and the Industrial Schools were eventually merged into Approved Schools.

By a second Industrial Schools Act of 1861 children found wandering and destitute with no apparent means of support apart from petty crime ('vagrant') could also be committed even if they had not become liable to a prison sentence. Some of these were very young children well below the age of criminal responsibility.[3] In addition, Poor Law Guardians could apply for a magistrate's order for any child who was unmanageable in the workhouse, and so could parents whose children were beyond control.

Industrial Schools aimed to surround such children, sometimes for the first time in their lives, with examples of honest, hardworking adults. Punctuality and concentration would be taught

Newcastle Old Gaol, 1822. Child criminals over the age of seven could, in theory, be sent to gaol.

by means of manual work on the premises as well as by three hours or so of schooling each day. These were to be boarding schools as far as possible, because a school's good influence during the day might be wholly lost if a child returned each night to vicious and criminal surroundings. Pupils were to be fed enough to keep them healthy but not given better food than a working man's child. There was public concern from the outset lest the children of thieves and idlers be given an easier childhood than those of honest working parents. This concern extended also to Ragged Schools, which we will examine later.

Except in the case of schools founded by churches for their own believers, Industrial Schools were not to be denominational, that is, they were not to be an expression of the Church of England. The Bible must be taught but not the Creeds or Catechism. Children would attend services each Sabbath at the nearest church of their own faith. Although it was expected that most children would board, provision was made for those who had a good 'outside' home with parents or others to spend their nights there. However, daily attendance at the school was as compulsory for these pupils as for the boarders.[4] Compulsory schooling at that time was unusual; indeed it was the element of compulsion which tended to put the schools into a 'juvenile prisons' category rather than an educational one.

Some Industrial Schools for boys were in fact Training Ships which had been established in the previous century. HMS *Wellesley*, berthed at South Shields, took a number of boys from Newcastle. These ship schools had an extra criterion of selection, namely whether the boy was suited to life at sea. The boys however were all young 'delinquents' of one sort or another.

Described thus the schools might seem no more than a soft arm of the penal system but they were much more than this. To begin with, they were not conceived by the penal system,

10

Sandgate, Newcastle, 1800. Destitute and criminal children lived in places like this.

although used by it. The schools were started by high-minded individuals and funded by philanthropic subscription and fees. When the Government started to use them for juvenile offenders it made an annual per capita grant. This varied over time, but we know that in 1867 it was £13.[5] In addition, constant and tireless efforts were made to get parents (where they could be found) to pay the fees necessary towards a child's upkeep and education, but this was often a vain endeavour. The system was hamstrung by the fact that no child could be excluded for non-payment of fees: provided he conformed to the rules he was bound to be kept on for the period of his 'sentence'. This meant that if the parents would not pay the fees someone else must: this was usually either the civic authority or the Government itself.

The philanthropists who founded Industrial Schools had, like most of the nineteenth-century English intelligentsia, huge faith in education. One might almost see them as expressing Plato's belief that no one does wrong knowingly: if people, especially children, could learn enough of the right things, they would be good. Additionally the Puritan belief in the saving power of work was still mightily prevalent. The Industrial Schools were one example among many in the nineteenth century that combined Platonic idealism with the Protestant work ethic. They were a late expression of the Enlightenment idea that society could be cured of its ills by rational arrangement and planned institutions. They embodied that burning moral sense which marked the Age of Reform.

Children committed to Industrial Schools would work as well as learn, their founders planned. Some of these founders hoped the work would be real, productive work resulting in goods and services to be sold on the open market; this proved on the whole an ambition too far. But older boys could be apprenticed out at the school's discretion and arrangement, whilst still

HMS *Wellesley*, a Training Ship berthed at South Shields which was also an Industrial School.

remaining pupils. The schools were intended to be at least partially self-supporting, and some certainly attained this goal sporadically. The very lowest expectation was that the boys and girls would turn out as honest citizens and not be a drain on society.[6]

Industrial Schools were not the only flower of Victorian high-mindedness, of course, nor even the only result of the attempt to deal with juvenile crime. Reformatories, regulated and certified in 1854, were for those, twelve to sixteen years old on entry, who had served a prison sentence and were therefore felt to be 'hardened'. Reformatories, as the name suggests, aimed at character reformation, but they also had a punishment aspect. Physical conditions there were more spartan than in the Industrial Schools and the discipline harsher. They were usually built away from towns, which gave an impression of segregation from ordinary life: Industrial Schools by contrast were set up in the very centres and residential areas of towns. Visitors were frequent and there was much coming and going, as will be shown later. The Reformatory Schools Acts of 1854 and 1855 showed their penal role: criminals under sixteen could be sentenced to fourteen days imprisonment followed by two to five years in a Reformatory. As we have said, these entry requirements were to prove a handicap as time went on.

Like the Industrial Schools, Reformatories relied heavily on manual work as a means of character training. But so did many other kinds of schools: there was a strong belief in the good influence of manual work. Workhouse children worked too, alongside adults, the hope being (again) that their labours would earn money on the open market and thus teach young residents to support themselves in the outside world. This hope was soon abandoned with regard to adults. It was realised that if paupers had been capable of producing goods wanted by the market they would not have been paupers in the first place.

What Were the Ragged and Industrial Schools?

Ragged Schools, which had become widespread some decades before the Industrial Schools, were another charitable enterprise which believed in both manual work and education as the way to save abandoned children. They were unusual in that their first founder had been not a rich philanthropist but a shoemaker, John Pounds, a Portsmouth man who was living in London when he started his school. At the turn of the eighteenth into the nineteenth century all towns swarmed with neglected, criminal and exploited children for reasons already given. Schools for poor children did exist but they had the right to refuse admission; wild, semi-criminal street children, some of whom had been in prison, most of whom never washed and would not sit still, were not admitted. Parish and Charity schools were for the respectable working class, as the advertisement for an Infants' School in Newcastle makes clear. Moreover, all schools charged fees: those for the poor kept their fees within the means of working parents, but nevertheless they had to be paid. But street children's parents would certainly not pay to send them to school; indeed it was in their interest to keep them on the streets. John Pounds started by taking some of these children into his house for a few hours a day and teaching them the three 'R's. As an inducement to come and learn each child was given a hot potato. Crucially, Pound did not expect the parents to pay anything; in this he was as much realist as philanthropist. The lack of requirement for payment made his little school quite different from others founded and run by charity. His example was quickly followed all over the country and in 1844 the Ragged School Union was formed under the chairmanship of the Earl of Shaftesbury. One of the most famous Ragged Schools was set up and run by Mary Carpenter in Bristol. The Newcastle School we are concerned with here started life as a Ragged School.[7]

At Ragged Schools children were fed – not generously but regularly – and taught the three 'R's. Some gave instruction in work skills, some provided beds and dormitories. They were thus very similar to the Industrial Schools which followed close on their heels except they did not attempt to get financial contributions from parents and in the matter of attendance: Ragged School children were under no compulsion to attend. No child went to a Ragged School on a magistrate's order in lieu of prison, although some of them had been in prison. Industrial School children were under such a compulsion. Moreover the recently-formed Council of Education retained the sole right to examine and certify Ragged Schools throughout their history: they, unlike the Industrial Schools, were never the province of the Home Office.

Ragged Schools received annual per capita Government grants but the amount varied widely over time in accordance with the public mood on Government support for delinquent children. For that matter the per capita grant given to Industrial Schools also varied, though less widely, and for the same reasons. The two kinds of school, Ragged and Industrial, dealt with exactly the same kind of children even though their entry criteria were different, and many schools which began life as Ragged Schools became Industrial Schools in addition. Both Ragged and Industrial Schools, and indeed the Reformatories, retained the legal right to refuse admission to any particular child, even if they rarely used it.

Between 1857 and 1860 the teaching in Industrial Schools was answerable only to the Council of Education and it was this body which granted certification. But in 1861, for a mixture of ideological and administrative reasons, it was brought under the overall control of the Home Office, in line with the teaching given in the Reformatories.

Government grants to both Ragged and Industrial schools were intended to cover half the rent of buildings, an allowance towards teachers' salaries[8], and basic school meals; this meant that the other half of the rents plus salaries of ancillary staff and cost of equipment, clothes, bedding, fuel, plumbing and maintenance had to be found from voluntary subscriptions. Neither type of school was a charge on the Parish Rates like the workhouses; they were not part of the Poor

Law. However, a workhouse could itself send children to an Industrial School for being beyond their own control, in which case the fees were paid by the workhouse, i.e. the money came from the Poor Law budget. In practice, parishes and civic authorities made permanent annual contributions to both Ragged and Industrial schools within their boundaries.

Industrial Schools' links to the penal system were indirect even within the Home Office remit. There was the annual grant, and there were twice-yearly inspections by Home Office personnel: inspections of educational attainment as well as physical care and conformity to legal requirements. Prison authorities, in a further Act of 1866, were given powers to contribute towards 'establishing, enlarging, or maintaining an Industrial School', and in Parliamentary Acts of 1872, 1874 and 1877 these powers were increased. But they did not themselves set about constructing such schools up and down the country. Private charity, including, as noted, large civic donations, founded and ran the schools initially. They could apply for the certification 'Industrial School' – and the Government grant that went with it – if they met certain criteria. This explains why many of them began life under other designations, often 'Ragged School' or 'Boys' Refuge'.

We might wonder why the Government made grants to schools founded and managed by private groups or individuals and financed by public benevolence. And why should the Government inspect them as well? Schools were already inspected by their own governing bodies. A.S. Bishop, in *The rise of a central authority for English education*, says: '..[S]tate Inspectorate – firmly established in several continental countries – had already been introduced into England through the 1833 Factory Act and the New Poor Law of 1834' . These Acts touched on education because there was concern that child workers in the northern mill-towns might be working hours so long as to leave no time for education. Regulations were laid down for minimum hours of schooling each day for each child, and factories informed they would be inspected to ensure compliance. As for Government grants, Treasury grants-in-aid for educational bodies had been going for centuries, since the days of the Protectorate in fact. In the nineteenth century the young Queen Victoria, expressing 'deep concern at the want of instruction observable among the poorer classes of her subjects' suggested, via Lord John Russell, that 'a Board or Committee [be founded] for the consolidation of all matters affecting the Education of the People [which] which should be entrusted with the application of any sums which may be voted by Parliament for the purpose of Education in England and Wales.'[9] As we shall see, the Queen (and she was not alone) was mistaken about the lack of instruction amongst the poorest children.

It must be remembered that until the 1870 Act which established universal, mostly free elementary education, all schools charged fees, usually low ones, and parents were expected to pay unless they were paupers. The one exception, as we have seen, were the Ragged Schools. Over their whole history the Industrial Schools struggled to get parents to pay the fees but it was a losing battle. The requirement of fees put Industrial Schools into a 'schools' category, but the process of committing children there for a sentence of time put them into a 'semi-prison' category. Children were committed for varying lengths of time, but not beyond their sixteenth birthday except in special circumstances. Removal of a child, by the school itself or by anyone else, was a serious matter requiring permission from the Home Office. An absconding child could in theory be sent to a Reformatory. And removal of a child by an adult without Home Office permission was an offence punishable by a fine.

Compulsory attendance marked out Industrial School and Reformatories as different from other schools, in which attendance was a matter partly of parents' day-to-day wishes. But Industrial Schools were like other schools, and unlike penal establishments, in that they could

An early Ragged School.

refuse to admit any child. It is indicative of the schools' mixed and shifting connotations that seven separate Acts about them were passed in twenty-three years, each cancelling some previous provisions and setting out new ones.

Like workhouses, Industrial Schools were meant to be physically comfortable: warm and dry with enough plain food (we will consider the diet in detail later), water closets, and hot water for bathing. Most children there almost certainly fared better physically than they would have done on the streets. But there was a great deal of discipline and regimentation – we will look at a typical day later – which street children must have found onerous, at least to start with. Strict timetabling was considered character forming; the children did get some free time but not much and only at certain hours. The nearest modern equivalent is probably life in the army.

Some Victorian reformers thought Industrial Schools, like the harder Reformatories for older children, should retain an element of punishment as well as working to reform character. Such men and women believed in the concept of sin, i.e. conscious willed wrongdoing. To them, as to many theologians since early Christian times, it was the capacity for sin that marked out full humanity. Animals could not sin, nor could babies or imbeciles; everyone else could. Children above the age of reason who had deliberately broken the law should therefore be treated as wrongdoers and punished, albeit with respect for their tender years.[10]

The clash between those two schools of thought partly explains the change of control of the Industrial Schools in the early years. The schools attracted opposition from the outset. A leader in *The Times* of January 1873 complained that 'the practice of relieving parents of responsibility by removing all vagrant children into Industrial Schools would end in casting upon the State the duty of supporting and launching in the world all the children of the poor.' The writer goes on to say that other European countries which gave Government grants to charitable boarding schools for street children had found this to be true. It also pointed out that removing the penalty of a child's upkeep from the parents had taken away a crucial deterrent against having illegitimate children. These were practical, pragmatic objections, although questions of parental responsibility cover more than just financial matters: morality and philosophy are involved too.

The ideological struggle did not show as a simple split between educationists on the one hand and the penal system on the other . The same struggle went on in prisons themselves, especially those for young offenders. Parkhurst prison on the Isle of Wight had introduced humane new practices for juveniles including workshops and market gardening years before the Industrial Schools started. These programmes, won in the teeth of the traditionalist camp, were widely applauded. It thus came as a shock and an embarrassment to all parties when Mary Carpenter, one of the great pioneers of Ragged Schools, denounced Parkhurst without having seen its recent reforms as an evil contrast to the schools she proposed.[11]

Industrial Schools lasted not much more than eighty years under that designation, some considerably less. By the Children and Young Persons Act of 1932, they and the Reformatories were redesignated as Approved Schools. But Industrial Schools had been flailing financially for many years. 1870 brought the Forster Education Act establishing Boards of Education over most of the country. These Board Schools over time rendered unnecessary the many Charity Schools which existed (though that was not their original intention) and removed one ideological prop (namely, educating destitute children) from the Industrial Schools' *raisons d'etre,* leaving only the penal function. Since Board Schools were funded from general taxation, people who had previously been donors to Ragged and Industrial Schools had second thoughts. Why should they pay twice to educate the children of the poor: once through donations and now through taxation? Voluntary contributions fell off drastically. By the 1890s and into the turn of the new century Industrial Schools were accepting pupils well outside their original remit, so long as funding came with them. Many of these were persistent truants from the new Board Schools. Truants were something new.

The 1870 Act did not make elementary education compulsory but gave local authorities the power to do so. Those that exercised this power (Newcastle was one) soon found themselves with a huge truancy problem. Until then, sending children to school had been a matter of daily parental choice (except of course for the Industrial Schools and Reformatories); children had home duties and sometimes paid work; education was a luxury for easy times. Among criminals and semi-criminals a worse attitude prevailed: many were positively hostile to the idea of their children going to school every day when they could be out making, or taking, money. Because both respectable parents and criminal or neglectful ones had the right to order their children's days it must sometimes have been hard to distinguish between the two classes. It was normal to see streets full of children going about their business, whether laudable or nefarious. In the early days of Industrial Schools any person suspicious or concerned about any child on the street could take him or her before a magistrate. Later, 'Children's Agents' were appointed by the various civic authorities.

As for compulsory attendance at school, children themselves were not necessarily enthusiastic, a fact which remains true today. It took generations, starting from the 1870s, to establish the idea of compulsory education in the public mind. Meanwhile, what was to be done with these truants?

Some were sent to existing Industrial Schools, but where the number of truants was great, local authorities built Day Industrial Schools to cope with them and also with such 'street Arab' children as could not be committed into the boarding Industrial Schools. The 1870 Act also granted the new Board of Education the same powers of contribution towards establishing, enlarging and maintaining Industrial Schools as the prison service already had. In addition it could start Industrial Schools *ab initio*. Board of Education Inspectors would henceforth carry out their own inspections of the schools in addition to those by the Home Office. This was to ensure standardisation of teaching throughout the whole child population. The effect on Industrial Schools was to bring them under a dual guardianship. Industrial Schools of both sorts, boarding and the new Day schools, remained answerable to the Home Office. Therefore, removal of a child by anyone, including itself, was a serious matter which could in theory lead to placement in a Reformatory (for a child of the appropriate age) or a fine (for a culpable adult). In practice children who absconded of their own free will simply had their 'sentence' at the Industrial School extended. Truants were thus made aware that they risked a lot if they persisted in their waywardness.

The presence of many Board School truants altered the ethos of the original (boarding) Industrial Schools, fluid though this had always been. But at least they staved off financial crisis for a good many years, since Government and local authorities would always in the end pay fees that parents would not. As philanthropic donations dropped off, truants became for many Industrial Schools their most reliable form of income. But trouble of a different sort was growing, as the remit of Reformatories came increasingly to be questioned.

Reformatories, it will be recalled, were for children aged over twelve on entry who had served a prison sentence. One gets the impression that the founders had assumed that the younger the child the greater the innocence, and that there would be no 'perishing and dangerous children' (to use Mary Carpenter's phrase) over twelve who had not been to prison. This was not the case. There were many older children among the wild swarms who, whilst living on the edge of the law, had not been to prison but were in danger of doing so. Their need was exactly the same as the younger children's: they needed a secure environment where their physical needs would be met and where they would be taught the three 'R's, discipline, and work habits: in other words a Reformatory or something like it. Magistrates, realising this, often deliberately sentenced these young offenders to a short spell in prison in order to qualify them for a Reformatory place! In 1899 the stipulation of a prior prison sentence was finally abolished. But by then the whole subject of juvenile crime was under discussion. There were other criticisms of the Reformatories.

Since Catholic emancipation in 1829 the Roman Catholic church had been allowed to set up and run its own schools, including semi-penal establishments like Reformatories and Industrial Schools. In Catholic Reformatories girls could be committed not simply for lawbreaking or 'vagrancy' but also, on the request of their parents or parish priest, for 'immoral behaviour'. This led to the flagrant injustice of punishing girls (i.e. sending them to the Reformatory) for acts committed against them by men.

Why should faults in the Reformatories affect Industrial Schools? Because in the public mind the two were seen as junior and senior versions of the same thing; both were referred to popularly as 'Home Office Schools'. The perception of Industrial Schools as just junior Reformatories deepened after elementary education itself, including education of the poorest children, became general as the result of parliamentary Acts. For these reasons, plus administrative ones, it was decided to merge Industrial Schools and Reformatories. This was done by means of the Children and Young Persons Act of 1932.

Over the years the Home Office inspection of Industrial Schools changed, most markedly with regard to the sexes. In 1913 it was recommended, and later became mandatory, that the schools be inspected every three months, not six, and that at least one Inspector should be a woman.[12] Women Inspectors were far readier than men to notice faults in bathing arrangements, provision of bedding, available play areas and the general organisation of the childrens' day. The Newcastle Industrial Schools, whose history will be traced in this study, received a damning report from one woman Inspector in 1909. Her severest criticism was that girls at the school were little more than household drudges for the teachers and the boys. Their 'industrial training' – never anything but housework and laundry – took precedence over their education, so that classes were fitted into any slots of available time. The girls, tired in the evening from their hard day, had to choose between an hour's leisure and an hour's schooling.

How many Industrial Schools were there? D.H. Thomas of Newcastle-upon-Tyne Polytechnic (now Northumbria University) published in 1986 a list of all Industrial Schools and Reformatories certified by the Home Office between 1854 and 1933 (the date at which the two merged) in England, Scotland and Wales.[13] Of course not all the schools on the list were in existence for the whole seventy-nine years. One in Birmingham lasted only ten years: some had even shorter lives. Moreover, the designations of many of them chopped and changed as they came now into one category – and its accompanying grant – now into another. The following figures are extracted from D.H. Thomas' list and include only those Industrial Schools which were boarding schools, i.e. examples of the principle at its most realized. But there were many Day Industrial Schools towards the end of the century, perhaps half as many as boarding schools, most of them, as has been described, dealing with truants from the Board Schools. I have not excluded Industrial Schools founded expressly for handicapped children, two dozen or so of which were in operation at one time or another. Thus the numbers of boarding Industrial Schools during the years in question were as follows: 113 for boys, 111 for girls, 46 mixed. In addition there were sixteen Training Ships which took on boys qualifying for an Industrial School as well as those sentenced to a Reformatory. For comparison here are Thomas' numbers for Reformatories: forty-eight for boys, thirty-three for girls, and three mixed. It may be worthwhile here to point out that Newcastle's Industrial Schools were not the only ones in the north-east; Sunderland for instance had two, one for each sex.

Did the Industrial Schools succeed in their grand ambition of breaking the links between poverty, ignorance and crime? In a grand sense, obviously not, but they seem to have done some good. Gertrude Tuckwell, in *The State and its Children* (1894) gives interesting figures: '3,964 children left the Industrial Schools of England and Scotland in 1891; 129 emigrated, 450 went to sea, 99 enlisted. Besides these, 87 were discharged as diseased, 39 had to be sent to Reformatories from Industrial Schools, 105 died, and 28 absconded. The percentage taken of those who have passed through their entire term of Industrial School life, deducting that is to say those who have been committed to Reformatories or discharged for disease, gives 86 per cent success in after-life.'[14] Miss Tuckwell admits there are some children for whom no follow-up record exists, but I think it must be admitted that her figures are quite impressive. Records of the life after school of the boys of the Newcastle Industrial and Ragged Schools, which will be shown later, are equally praiseworthy.

The Government itself in the 1884 Report on Reformatories and Industrial Schools said: 'The effect of the system of certified schools, established by these enactments, upon juvenile and adult crime, has on the whole been very satisfactory. They are credited, we believe justly, with having broken up the gangs of young criminals in the larger towns; with putting an end to the training of boys as professional thieves; and with rescuing children fallen into crime from becoming habitual or hardened offenders, while they have undoubtedly had the effect of preventing large numbers of children from entering a career of crime. These conclusions are confirmed by statistics of the juvenile commitments to prison in England and Wales since 1856 (two years after the passing of the first English Reformatory Act, and one year before the first Industrial Schools Act). In 1856 the number of the commitments was 13,981; in 1866 it was 9,356; in 1876 it was 7,138. Since that time the number has regularly decreased, and had fallen in 1881 to 5,483. [A footnote however states that the 1882 figure was 5,700 – a slight rise]. [W]hereas in the quinquennial period of 1855-9 one sentence of penal servitude was inflicted to every 7,438 of the population, the proportion steadily decreased, until in the year 1881 there was only one sentence to every 17,028.'

Did the schools work as economically self-sufficient units as their more utopian founders hoped? Again, no, but many managed to be self-sufficient from time to time in some goods and services, usually in their early years, and some established successful contracts with local firms for the firms' work to be done at the school. This was especially true of laundry, carried out commercially in some girls' schools. The Newcastle Schools did not do commercial laundry but tailoring and shoemaking were performed on contract in the boys' school in the 1880s. The school workshops produced a variety of goods over the years; unfortunately, the most reliable profits came from sacks and chopped firewood. This was not the work training the founders had had in mind. But whatever their financial results the schools certainly gave an unknown number of children some safe and secure years and perhaps an advantage in the world of work.

It must be stressed, however, that there was much dissent over the schools and just as in any other age opinions were not unanimous. We shall encounter contrary arguments in the course of the history of the Newcastle School. But the atmosphere of progress, almost utopianism, that characterised the time tended to carry all before it. Belief in the power of education was particularly strong.

But how had the schools functioned on the day-to-day dinners-and-drains level, which is the level all high-flown theories must descend to if they are to be more than ideas? What did the children think of the schools? Are there any records of what they thought? Were they well fed or were they often ill?

This investigation of the Newcastle Ragged and Industrial Schools restricts itself to just that. There were two other Industrial Schools in Newcastle in the second half of the nineteenth century: St James' (also known as the Chadwick Memorial School) for boys, and St Elizabeth (also known as Ashburton House) for girls. These were never Ragged Schools and were also Roman Catholic enterprises, not typical of the new attitudes of the Victorian age. A Ragged School which became also an Industrial School is more typical, like the numerous Refuges founded by benefactors up and down the country which followed the same course. Schools which started with one function and went on to include another give opportunities to look at overlapping ambitions.

Why did so many institutions get themselves registered as Industrial Schools? One big factor was money: the Government per capita grant for Industrial Schools was greater and more reliable than its grants to other institutions. There was no choice for child or parent about attendance

Quayside 1885

at an Industrial School; such schools were in that respect comparable to prisons and therefore deserved a similar per capita grant. However, the Industrial Schools' larger grant did not at any time cover their expenses. The chief sources of income remained fees and philanthropy. For instance, Newcastle Borough Council (as it then was) made regular annual grants to the Newcastle Ragged School and continued to do so when it became a certified Industrial School. They made similar grants to the Roman Catholic institutions. Other contributors could be private individuals, commercial firms, professional associations and the like. Fees were a constant trouble at all Industrial Schools: efforts to claim them from parents were often fruitless and many cases ended with the local authority paying. Ragged Schools, of course, did not charge fees. A combined Ragged and Industrial School like the Newcastle one must have been a trial to its accountant.

It will be noticed that I write sometimes of the Newcastle 'school' and sometimes of 'schools'. In theory there were two separate schools: the boys', which opened first, and the girls', which followed shortly afterwards. Both shared the same premises in the early years. With the move to Jubilee Road the girls' quarters were to some extent separate, but throughout most of the schools' history the girls' manual work consisted of washing the boys' clothes and cleaning their quarters. This eventually led to strong criticism from a Government Inspector and during the next few years the girls' school, or girls' part of the school, emptied and closed. Throughout I shall use either 'school' or 'schools' as the sense demands.

What Were the Ragged and Industrial Schools?

The school's Annual Reports, and other documents, suggest that Industrial Schools, despite failing to fulfil their somewhat utopian remit, were probably a good thing. Information gathered twice-yearly by the Home Office Inspectors shows that the children's health was good compared with the general child population, and that epidemics were rare. Punishments were humane by the standards of the time and rarely took the form of caning or strapping.[15] The Annual Reports quote letters from old boys and girls saying how happy they had been at school although we should bear in mind that children who had been miserable would not have written back. The letters show that at least some of them had a happy childhood in Industrial Schools. And what became of them out in the world? R.S. Watson, in his 1867 pamphlet on the Newcastle Schools, speaking of the subsequent fortunes of old scholars, cites one who, after attending the University of Aberdeen, became a minister of the Church of Scotland. He says two others are masters of thriving businesses in the town (Newcastle), two are assistants at doctors' surgeries, three work in chemical laboratories, one is an overseer in a large spinning mill, two have 'during the past year, sailed from the Tyne as mate of vessels whilst several have risen to be non-commissioned officers in the army.' He then goes on to make what must be the *sine qua non* of testimonials to the schools' benevolent influence: 'not one lad who has passed through the School has been committed to prison for any offence whatever'. Mr Watson was writing when the schools were twenty years old; we must accept therefore that no old pupil had ended up in prison over that whole period. The fact that Mr Watson's report might be heavily biased in the schools' favour, since he was secretary of its Board of Governors, is counterbalanced by this statistic.

This study is offered as an exploration of a small piece of utopianism. What becomes of dreams when they materialise into flesh-and-blood children, bricks and mortar, dinners and drains? The Newcastle School seems, on the whole, to have been a force for good in at least some children's lives, the boys' lives at least. We shall see that it was less good for the girls, but only in the way that all Victorian society was less good for women and girls, especially if they were poor. It is interesting that the utopian founders of schools and refuges for neglected children were quite blind to their own assumption that girls were less important than boys. However, this study is not a feminist tract.

Newcastle in around 1840, a few years before the school opened.

Notes

1. The Aberdeen School of Industry, probably the first in Great Britain to approximate to the later Government-subsided Industrial Schools (the subject of this book) was founded in 1841 by public subscription. It was a day school which provided three meals a day for vagrant, begging and delinquent children, some of whom had served prison sentences. Attendance was *not* compulsory (no Magistrate's order then) but children who failed to attend even part-days missed the meal appropriate to that part of the day. Described in Sanders, W.B.: *Juvenile delinquents for a thousand years* (1973).

2. Determining the age of these children was difficult, as there was no compulsory registration of births until 1875 and even after that some children escaped registration. Magistrates were empowered to commit any child 'apparently' over seven and under fourteen years of age.

3. Gertrude Tuckwell, in *The State and its Children* (London, 1894) noted that one Industrial School, the Cottage Homes at Addlestone, had one child who had been admitted aged eighteenth months! (Quoted in Sanders, Wiley B. *op. cit.* p.305.)

4. Ibid.

5. R.J. Watson: *Industrial Schools* [pamphlet] Newcastle, 1867, printed at Newcastle Ragged and Industrial Schools.

6. Anonymous article on Ragged Schools in the *Newcastle Daily Chronicle* Feb. 15 1877.

7. Newcastle Ragged and Industrial Schools started as Ragged Schools, and received annual subscriptions from Newcastle Borough Council from the outset. When the schools received their legal certification as 'Industrial', the Borough Council made an annual contribution to them of £42 0s 0d. To the Roman Catholic Industrial Schools, St James' (also known as Chadwick Memorial School) and St Elizabeth's (also known as Ashburton House) the Council's annual donation was £26 5s 0d.

8. HM Govt Industrial Schools Act 1861.

9. Letter of Lord John Russell to the President of the Committee in Council on Education. Quoted in Bishop, *op. cit.* pp.19-20.

10. Blackstone, *op.cit.*

11. House of Commons Select Committee on Criminal and Destitute Children, 21 May 1852, pp. 101-103.

12. HM Govt Home Office Report on Reformatories and Industrial Schools, 1913.

13. Thomas, D.H. *op. cit.*

14. Tuckwell, Gertrude, *op. cit.*

15. HM Govt Report 1913, *op. cit.* See also Annual Reports of Newcastle Ragged and Industrial Schools, which include favourable reports from Government medical officers. For example, Newcastle Ragged and Industrial Schools Annual Report 1901 says that discipline is chiefly by 'forfeiture of privileges, and loss of good conduct marks, which earn pecuniary rewards'. See also Newcastle Ragged and Industrial Schools Log Book of Punishments for the 1880s.

2

Schooling and Literacy in the Nineteenth Century

E.G. West in *Education and the Industrial Revolution* claimed that nineteenth-century education has been misrepresented, especially in the popular mind, by Dickens. Anecdotal evidence from my own family inclines me to agree with him.

My maternal great-grandfather, a first generation 'immigrant' to the Durham coalfields from the Cornish clay mines, was well read and a fluent writer. He became a Methodist lay minister whilst remaining a coalminer. My grandfather, his son, died before I could ask him about his father's schooling; he made me aware though that his father, whilst considered quite a clever man, was by no means a prodigy in his community. There, it was a matter of shame *not* to be able to read and write rather than of pride to know how to. Since my grandfather was born in the 1870s his father must certainly have received his schooling before the 1870 Education Act.

E.G. West, using the few original unbiased records available,[1] says a reasonable estimate would be that, in the 1830s, between two thirds and three quarters of the *working class* could read, though not necessarily write as well [my emphases]. A detail he quotes serves the present study nicely: in 1840 an unbiased test of literacy was taken by Northumberland and Durham miners. In one particular colliery, from a total of 843 pitmen, 445 could both read and write (i.e. over half) and a further 220 could read but not write. In other words, 79 per cent of these miners could read, and this in 1840 when all schooling had to be paid for and children went to work at an early age. Although this was the 'best' colliery the others were not signally worse.

The Revd W.C. Osborn, in *The Cry of 10,000 Children, or Cruelty towards the Young* (1860), records some surprising figures regarding the most wretched children in the country: 'In the three years ending September 1856, the juvenile delinquent population of England and Wales under sixteen years of age were represented by an annual average of about 15,000 committals to our common prisons: about one half of these children were orphans, or deserted by their parents, 43 per cent could neither read not write. About 45 per cent could read and write but imperfectly, and about 15 per cent had the ability to read and write, [o]ne sixth of the whole were twelve years or under.'[3] In one sense this information is shocking but looked at another way a figure of almost 60 per cent who could read at some level shows that the popular belief (then and now) that all destitute children in the nineteenth century were illiterate is wrong. Significantly, in 1856, the year the Revd Osborn studied, Industrial Schools were on the point of receiving Government certification, and Ragged Schools were well established. They were obviously

Colliers were more literate than is generally realised. Probably many of their wives were too.

contributing to rising standards of literacy. A more startling piece of evidence lies in a letter from William Augustus Miles to Lord John Russell in 1837. At this date Ragged Schools were in their infancy and Industrial Schools few and far between and not yet formally acknowledged. One would expect therefore that hardly any child delinquents could read – not so. Mr Miles is reporting on children in prison: 'There is a library in the boys' ward at Newgate: amongst [the] other books there are a few containing history and travels, and it is with these latter books that the boys are delighted; they read them with eagerness, and the more illiterate boys will subscribe portions of food to engage the services of a boy to read them aloud. [Some who] did not know their letters when they came to prison were enabled to read before they left it.'[4] This would seem to contradict later criticisms that many children classified as 'able to read' could in fact only stumble through a few verses of Scripture they had learned by heart.

The Royal Commission on Popular Education of 1861 (the Newcastle Commission) reported that the average length of schooling for children in the late 1850s was 5.7 years, which, taking into account the extended education of the upper classes, suggests that most children got some schooling, including, as we have seen, over half of the most destitute.[2]

Dickens, like other followers of Jeremy Bentham, favoured Government action to right the 'wrong' of the illiteracy of the poor and the bad state of private schools. 'Illiteracy' of the poor we have looked at; what about the scandalous private schools? Places like Dotheboys Hall certainly did exist but were by no means typical. Before the 1870 Act there was a huge variety of schools, all 'private' in the sense that there were no state schools; all charged fees of some sort. It is not surprising that bad schools existed, any more than it is surprising today that 'sink' schools exist.

Before looking at the variety of schools available in the mid-nineteenth century we should perhaps lay down some markers: not until 1870 were state-funded schools provided universally; not until an Act of 1881 was elementary education compulsory and not until 1891 was state schooling free for all children.

In the mid-nineteenth century fees for children's education were the norm although, as has been pointed out, fees for most schools were affordable by working people. Families fallen on hard times could have the fees paid by the parish or other bodies. Pauper children in the workhouse had schooling provided at public expense either on site in the workhouse or at the new Union Schools ('Union' here refers to unions of parishes for purposes of Poor Law administration).

At the other end of the social scale from the workhouse were the aristocracy and gentry. Almost without exception they employed tutors and governesses for their children. For the great mass of the population between these two extremes there were, by the late 1840s, many schools available. I shall describe them not in date order of their foundation but in terms of their use by different classes of society, starting with the richest. I had better make here the obvious point that not all schools taught the same things. Many assumed literacy in the children entering them: many in fact made it a condition of admission. The Grammar Schools taught the classical languages and literatures, so did some private academies. Only a few types of school taught the basic three 'R's. Good accounts of the main school types and their history can be found in S.J. Curtis's *History of Education in Great Britain* and W.B. Stephens' *Education in Britain 1750-1914*. Much of the following detail arises from these studies.

Grammar Schools

These date from Tudor times or earlier. Their original purpose, to educate clever sons of the poor for entry to the professions, was subsumed by the middle classes who had taken them over and who might or might not intend their sons for the professions. There were no girls' Grammar Schools, but some had infant departments which taught the three 'R's to younger children.

Private Academies

These came in every shape and competence. Some, like the Bruce Academy in Newcastle-upon-Tyne, were first class and locally famous. Others were not. The report of an 1858 Commission on private education – which could equally well have applied to earlier decades – condemned the premises of some as 'injurious to health' and many of the teachers as '...too poor, too ignorant, too feeble, too sickly, too unqualified in any or every way...' to be fit for schoolkeeping. So Dotheboys Hall was a realistic creation, but far from the whole picture. Most private academies only took children who could already read and write. Despite this, and despite the enormous variations in standards, these schools were used at least some of the time by people of all classes: all, that is, who wanted their children educated. Their great asset was their ubiquity: they far outnumbered all other kinds of school put together.

Dame Schools

These could be described as one kind of private academy, the difference being that the children they took could not read or write: teaching the basics to young children was the Dame Schools' function. They were usually run by a single elderly man or woman, and, like other private academies, varied enormously. By the mid-nineteenth century they were falling into disfavour and were being replaced, albeit piecemeal and sporadically, by charity- or corporation-sponsored Infant Schools. From medieval times Dame Schools had been the main providers of basic elementary education for young children, especially children of the poor.

Infant Schools

Various religious and civic bodies started Infant Schools in the mid-nineteenth century, following the lead of Robert Owen's pioneering New Lanark settlement in Scotland. They were first and foremost for the convenience of working parents; thus some of them took children from two years old. These youngest children were simply cared for, fed, and taught games, much as in a modern day nursery. At older ages they were taught the three 'R's and Bible stories.

Parish or Parochial Schools

In medieval and Reformation England all schooling had been the preserve of the Church, indeed its duty. The main purpose of early Church schools was to teach Christian doctrine, not the three 'R's. Curtis, in his history, says: '...the Church...through decrees of council and Episcopal charges, frequently reminded parish priests of their duty to maintain schools and to teach freely all children of the parish who came to them'. ['Freely' here means 'without bar or discrimination', not 'free of charge'.] But the three 'R's often were taught, as an aid to learning the Catechism. It was a matter for the parish priest. He need not himself have been the schoolmaster: in fact, priests were forbidden to do the teaching if someone better qualified was available. This ban itself suggests something other than the Catechism was being taught, for who could be better qualified to teach the latter than the priest? It is likely that some Dame Schools at least began as 'out-contracts' by parish priests. Teaching could take place, said the Church authorities, in any convenient place: no special building was needed.

But in Scotland after the Reformation every parish had an actual organised school attached to the Presbyterian Church of Scotland. Their clergy took their educational duties seriously and the children were well taught, in the three 'R's as well as Scripture. It is relevant to our present subject that some Scottish Parochial schools taught a wider curriculum, for instance practical subjects like land-surveying. In the early nineteenth century an effort was made in England to establish similar Parish Schools. The attempt was only half-successful and many became National Schools. Parish Schools were used by both the middle and working classes, especially in rural areas, because they were sometimes all that was available.

Roman Catholic and Nonconformist Church Schools

With religious emancipation in 1829 churches previously merely 'tolerated' were free to set up their own educational establishments. The only requirement for entry was that the pupil be of the designated faith, in theory at least. In practice they could and did exclude ragged, dirty and undisciplined children. Church schools of all denominations overlapped with Charity Schools. Churches could set up their own Industrial Schools.

National Schools

These were set up in England and Wales following the failure to establish universally Parish Schools, on the Scottish model, financed by Parish Vestries (administrative units for various laws as well as for church organisation). A Church of England initiative, the National Society for the Education of the Poor in the Principles of the Established Church, was the body that founded the schools. An additional stimulus to their founding was the dissenting churches' successful crusade to educate the poor with their British and Foreign Schools. The National Society's aim was to do its Christian duty to teach poor children without promoting social unrest. These conflicting aims caused unavoidable tension: once people can read they cannot be kept quietly 'in their place'.

British and Foreign Schools

These were a missionary enterprise by the nonconformist churches, who believed that spreading the Gospel must be done not only overseas but repeatedly here in England. Financed by private subscription chiefly from their own members nationwide and eschewing Treasury grants, they were intended for the otherwise untaught poor. Once again though, these schools also could and would refuse wild and filthy children.

Charity Schools

These mostly came into being in the early eighteenth century, resulting from private efforts of churches and especially of the Society for the Promotion of Christian Knowledge. Their interest was in children as potential believers and congregants: this marked them off from church schools proper which were for the children of existing church members. They were funded by donations from the churches that founded them and also from civic bodies of the towns in which they were set up. They were for children of the respectable working poor: children who were required to be clean, properly behaved, and as well clothed as the parents could afford. Newcastle-upon-Tyne had, according to a contemporary writer, a remarkable number of Charity Schools, 'exceeding most other towns'.

Sunday Schools

These had had their beginnings in the early eighteenth century, and by 1784 John Wesley was noting that they were springing up everywhere. In 1801 there were 2,290 Sunday Schools in the whole of Great Britain; by 1851 this had increased more than tenfold to 23,135. Of course this was the half-century in which the population exploded as well. Sunday Schools were originally for working children for whom Sunday was their only day off. Although religious bodies and religious people often ran them, Sunday Schools at first caused tensions in the churches because of their apparent breaking of the Third Commandment. However, a way around this was found and they flourished. In some parts of the country, the Potteries for instance, nine times as many children attended Sunday as day schools.[5] According to Briggs et al, in *Crime and Punishment in England*, one of the intended roles (perhaps covert) of Sunday Schools was the 'industrializing' of ex-agricultural workers newly arrived in towns. They say: 'It required many schools, and particularly Sunday Schools, with their lessoning in the industrial virtues of diligence, thrift, and especially 'regularity' to turn the people of the fields and the cottages into the people of the factories and the back streets'. In the course of time Sunday Schools were made available to younger children, supplementing and sometimes substituting for weekday education. And also in the course of time adults were admitted too. One could see the attraction they would have for poor parents: a child could work six days a week and still learn to read and write on Sundays. Sunday Schools charged small fees to cover their teachers' salaries. The buildings were erected with money from public subscription.

Informal schools in workplaces

The 1833 Factories Act, which prohibited the employment of children under eight years old, also required that children between nine and thirteen years receive part-time education, and that weekly proof of this be made available to Government Inspectors.[6] Such education could be either at local schools or at classes provided on the premises by factory owners. Indeed, from the very inception of large-scale industrial production of goods in the eighteenth century some factory and mill owners had provided education for their child workers. There are records of two such near Newcastle-upon-Tyne. The ironworks at Winlaton from 1717 had its own schoolmaster for its child workers, paid for by an employer/employee contribution scheme, and the Cambois colliery erected schools for its workers' children between 1840 and 1860.[7] (The Newcastle collieries, incidentally, never employed women underground). An interesting detail is revealed in the Factory Inspectors' official reports: apparently children on half-time teaching (three hours daily, the rest of the day being spent working) had attainments higher than those in full-time schooling!

Ragged Schools

We have seen something of these already. Established in the 1840s, they represented a national (not Church) effort to 'catch' poor children whose 'rude habits, filthy condition and want of shoes and stockings' meant that other schools would not accept them. We must constantly remind ourselves that at the time any school could refuse admission to a child it did not want. Ragged Schools were exceptional (and realistic) in charging no fees: there was no hope of such children's parents paying anything, even if they could be found. Like Charity Schools they were funded by donations, both private and civic. The Government made small grants towards the cost of feeding the children; indeed the schools were sometimes referred to as 'Feeding Schools'. They did not usually board and lodge their pupils, not, that is, unless they put themselves under the Home Office's remit and became Industrial Schools – which many did. In doing so of course they attracted the c. £13 per capita per annum Government grant. Most Ragged Schools taught some workskills and even some trades, so they were well placed to become accredited Industrial Schools.

Union Schools

These were established by unions of parishes (the administrative units of the Poor Law) shortly after the workhouses were reformed and reorganised. Up to that time pauper children had been taught on the premises: now special schools were founded for them. Although set up for workhouse children they often took other very poor children too. They were paid for out of the Poor Law budget.

Newcastle, *c.* 1840.

Night Refuges and Philanthropic Homes

I have put these last although every large town had one or two such establishments. Something has been said about them already. They were not first and foremost schools but, as their names suggest, safe lodging houses for boys and girls who had nowhere to sleep. Orphan children could be admitted to a workhouse if they met the strict criteria but many street children were not orphans, merely neglected. For schooling these children had the new Ragged Schools, but in their beginning Ragged Schools did not board pupils: they were day schools only. The Night Refuges gave such children a place to lodge. They were also used by boys and girls newly arrived in a strange town to look for work. Over time, in addition to board and lodging, some Refuges started to offer teaching: the three 'R's to such as had not mastered them, and workskills to all. Some Refuges were owned and run by churches, including St George's in Liverpool, a Roman Catholic foundation. Many of these, including St George's, became Industrial Schools. One can see the attraction of a regular guaranteed Government grant, even if small, to establishments which throughout their existence struggled to make ends meets.

Notes

1. West claims (convincingly) that many contemporary 'records' were biased because they were compiled by people whose idea of 'education' was peculiar, e.g. who did not consider a child 'taught' who had only learned the three Rs – and not the recordist's own brand of religion!

2. West, *op. cit.*

3. Osborn, W.C., *op. cit.* Quoted in Sanders, *op. cit.* p.268.

4. Quoted in Sanders, Wiley B. *op. cit.* p. 163.

5. From Stephens, W.B.: Education in Britain 1750-1914. (1998) p.25.

6. HM Govt *op. cit.*

7. Brewis, Elsdon W.: *The history and progress of education.* [pamphlet] Newcastle, Cambois colliery, 1881.

3
Schools in Newcastle: Beginning of the Ragged Schools

Speaking of the education of children in 1827, Eneas Mackenzie said in his *Descriptive and Historical Account of Newcasle-upon-Tyne and Gateshead*

'only one child in [three and a half] above five and not exceeding fifteen years of age, were destitute of instruction. Even this deficiency is not to be attributed so much to the want of means of instruction, as to the early age at which children are sent to the coalmines, and to the ignorance and depravity of the parents. These calculations shew that the counties of Newcastle and Northumberland are among the best educated in the country.'[1]

In fact the figure for children 'destitute of instruction' was probably even lower than Mackenzie's one in three-and-a-half. Children, especially poor children, did not necessarily go to school regularly and continuously. For a few months or a year their parents might 'spare' them and then they went to school. For the next few months or year they might be needed to earn money or care for babies whilst parents worked. A year later, perhaps in a different district or town, things might be easier and they could go to school again. If official figures for school attendance were collected during their time at home they would not be included. One cannot help being astonished at the level of literacy of poor children in the nineteenth century, including young criminals, evidence of which we have seen. Their sporadic schooling seems to have produced results almost as good as our present-day ten compulsory years in school.

During the nineteen years 1831 to 1850 the population of Newcastle-upon-Tyne (not including Gateshead) increased by almost 90 per cent to 87,000. Approximately 10,800 children between five and thirteen years old in 1850 were served by the following schools:

1 Grammar School
89 private academies, including an unknown number of Dame Schools
4 Infant Schools, which took children from two years old
2 Parish Schools
4 Roman Catholic or nonconformist Church Schools
7 National Schools (all ex-Church of England Parish Schools)
7 Charity Schools (including the Deaf and Dumb Institution)

An unknown number of Sunday Schools. Mackenzie gives an 1827 figure for
Newcastle and Gateshead combined of 21; by 1850 there would have been more.
2 on-site works schools (not actually within the town boundaries)
2 Ragged Schools. The first of them, for boys, opened in 1847.(The histories of these schools
we shall follow in detail.)
1 Union School, which also came into the category British and Foreign
School. (Probably a nonconformist enterprise for workhouse children)[2]

Of these institutions, only the Ragged Schools would accept wild, dirty, lawless children. The
figure of 'approximately 10,000' children between five and thirteen years old might include all,
some, or none of the 'street' children who swarmed in the town. Some of these might have had
their births recorded in the parish register, many would not. A proportion of street children
would be recent arrivals (vagrant parents by definition moved around a lot) but this would be
true of 'respectable' children too. The population had grown across all classes.

The previous centuries' travelling poor were now largely settled and in the process of upward
mobility. These were the respectable poor who clothed and fed their children and sent them to
school whenever finances allowed it. Some had even moved into the middle class. The 'street
children' were not theirs but the offspring of the more recent 'immigrants' described earlier,
together of course with the idlers and chancers thrown up by every generation. Certainly a
proportion of street children were not getting any schooling at all, partly on account of their
unmanageable behaviour. Mary Carpenter, writing of the Ragged School she opened in Bristol,
described the children as behaving more like young horses than human children, unaccustomed
to enclosed spaces and intolerant of restraint. But it was precisely to reach such children that
John Pounds had started his little Ragged School in the early part of the century.

On 2 July 1847 a group of philanthropists decided to start up a Ragged School in Newcastle.
They kept minutes of the meeting in question, and there we can read: '[T]he object is to
educate about 50 boys, between the ages of 6 and 14 years, who are not in circumstances to
attend a superior school; the education [shall] comprise Reading, Writing and Arithmetic with
instruction in the Holy Scriptures.' They go on to stipulate that one pennyworth of bread is to
be supplied daily to each pupil as an inducement to attend, and as a guard against thieving. The
premises of a Sunday School are to be rented for use on weekdays. A similar school for girls is to
be started as soon as means become available. A request has been made to the Ragged Schools
in Edinburgh for Mr Jack Murray, one of their best teachers, to spend a few days in Newcastle,
all expenses paid, to give advice on organisation and teaching. In the event on this first visit
Mr Murray stayed a week. Both he and the sponsors must have been pleased with each other
because when the school opened a month later he was appointed its first master. Like nearly all
Ragged Schools this was a day school: its hours were 9 a.m. until noon, and 2 p.m. to 4 p.m.

Those minutes make it clear that enough money had been raised to start the school, but that
continued and increasing donations would be needed to make it a success. Newcastle Borough
Council itself was an early and regular subscriber.

The accounts that follow draw heavily on the school's Board Minutes[3], Annual Reports,
special reports, Inspectors' reports and newspaper articles.

The school opened in mid-August of that year (1847) attended by much publicity and
goodwill. One of the governing body, Mr R.S. Watson, from whom we have quoted already,
had this to say about the original premises (writing twenty years later): 'On the 11th of August,
1847, a Ragged School was opened in Sandgate and in a few days forty boys were in attendance.
The district was an unhealthy one: the situation of the school was confined: the room itself very

low and dark'.[4] However, there were compensations, inspired no doubt by the evidence of a good work started and the wish that it should succeed. Presents of cheese were given so that the children could have a bread-and-cheese lunch rather than plain bread. The minutes of 16 September, when the school had been open a month, noted that in addition a gift of milk was being brought each morning, enabling the school to offer a bread-and-milk breakfast as well as a lunch.[5] The school was to be visited daily by one or another member of the governing board.

Shortly afterwards the local manufacturers Liddell and Dodds offered to employ boys, on the school premises, to make matchboxes. It will be recalled that the school had been intended to teach the three 'R's and Scripture, nothing more. The five hours of the school day were to be for learning. But the Board of Governors would have known that many Ragged Schools did practice manual work and that a few made money from it. A sub-committee therefore examined Liddell and Dodds' proposal and accepted it. By November many boys were making matchboxes. Since manual work required more energy than learning, the boys' food rations were increased. But the additional rations 'must not exceed twopence halfpenny worth per child per annum' because of the nationwide fear that children supported by charity might end up eating better than the children of poor but hard-working parents.

Matchbox-making was done by alternating groups of the older boys; at the end of the month they had completed 57 gross. The boxes were difficult to dry out and so a small stove was bought. By December the younger boys were employed about three hours daily 'teasing hair obtained from the coachmakers', payment being 9d per stone. Lofty theories about the character-forming influence of manual work lose some of their glory when the work turns out to be matchbox-making and hair-teasing. But this dull drudgery only took up part of the day; the rest of the time the boys had lessons and some leisure. And they did get two meals a day. On balance it was almost certainly a better life than the one they had known on the streets.

The Minutes for January 1848 make sad reading. The teacher, James Murray from Edinburgh, had died 'from the raging fever believed to have originated in the Irish famine'. He is praised as 'an intelligent and devoted young man, long accustomed to Sabbath School teaching' and the report continues: '[T]he unruly elements of which the school was composed quickly manifested themselves, but, in a very few weeks, by the admirable tact of the teacher, who knew well how to temper firmness with kindness, a marked change for the better was pleasingly apparent'. The Board of Governors are to appoint another teacher as soon as possible; in the meantime Mr Cowell, himself a member of the board, will do the teaching personally. These Minutes also note that that arrangements have been made to bring in supplies of clean second-hand clothes; many of the boys being poorly-clad and cold.

In 1848 the school moved to occupy part of Gibson Street Chapel which stood in a healthier position than Sandgate and in May the new teacher was appointed: a Mr James Short from London. The first public examination of the school, by a Council of Education Inspector, was held in September. This event was open to all subscribers and their guests as well as the full Board of Governors. The pupils were tested orally (no written exams yet), the teacher questioned, the premises inspected, the curriculum and meals discussed.[6] The school made a favourable impression on all present as well as receiving a good report from the Inspector. It was decided to admit girls as well as boys if the schoolroom could be partitioned and if the 'ladies' could appoint a female teacher. These 'ladies' would have been the wives, mothers or sisters of the male benefactors, or else wealthy women who subscribed in their own right.

Less than a year after opening the school changed its stated curriculum from 'the three 'R's plus Holy Scripture' to 'Reading, Writing, Arithmetic, a knowledge of the Holy Scriptures, and

Map of a part of Newcastle in 1844: the forth square along (reading left to right), second square down shows Sandgate, between and parallel to New Road and New Quay.

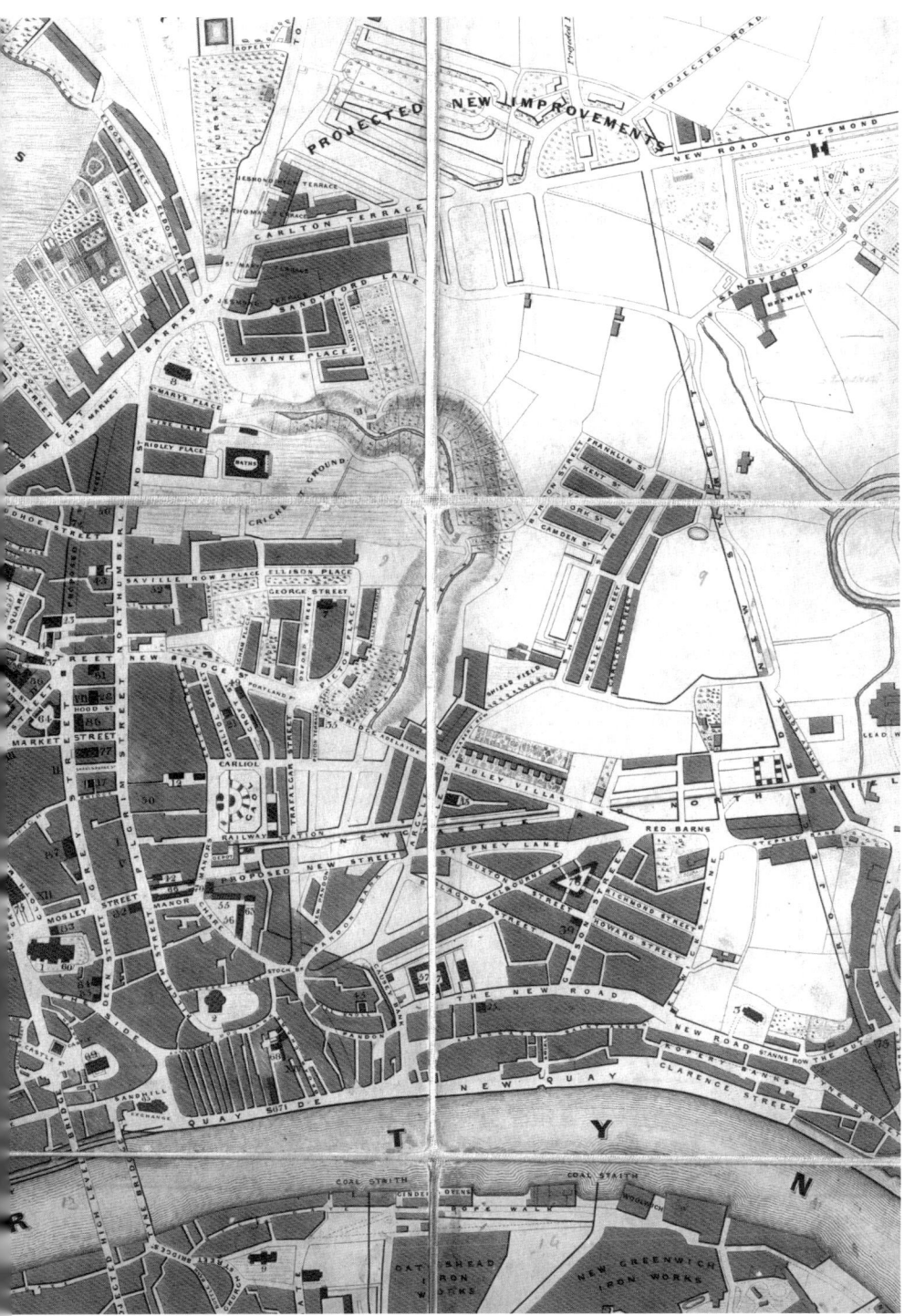

This is where the school started. Also shown are Gibson Street and New Road.

Grey Street, Newcastle 1860. Newcastle had a large and charitable middle class.

Moral and Industrial Training'. Here was a case of theory catching up with practice since most boys were already engaged on (low-grade) industrial training every day. A local benefactor had provided them all with working-smocks.

Early the following year the Girls' School began, unfortunately housed in the same room as the boys' schoolroom and separated only by a partition! The resulting chaos can be imagined. These were not biddable, quiet children; they were noisy, overactive and dirty. The idea of nearly a hundred of them in one room, albeit a large one divided by a partition, with only two teachers in charge, is daunting. At the earliest opportunity the Girls' School was moved to the 'western division of the chapel'.

By August 1849 that same large room, the boys' schoolroom, accommodated a workshop and shoemaker's shop, and eight boys were already making shoes under the direction of a qualified man. This was much more the kind of work envisaged by 'Industrial Training'. The school had improved in other ways too: washrooms and a bath had been installed. One senses that subscriptions were coming in steadily and in good amounts. After all, the school was still a novelty and its original benefactors still present and determined it should succeed. It would be a different story twenty years on.

Mr James Short would appear not to have been as good a teacher as the young deceased Mr Murray. Reports describe him as being 'anxious' for the 'moral and religious advancement of his charges', in which endeavour he has been '*in several instances* remarkably successful' [my italics]. A hope is expressed that 'his unsparing labours be crowned with a still more abundant blessing'. This surely is damning with faint praise.

Sandgate 1895. Still rough, long after the school had moved.

6

THE MASTER'S NOTES.

Boys' Ragged School, 11th August, 1849.

DURING the past year I have had much to contend with, but not more than was anticipated,—both master and pupils have had a conflict,—a war with the worst passions and habits of our nature. Looking back over the past year, I am pleased to find that the struggle has not been a vain one. On the one hand, as regards evil, the boys have unlearned some things, and, as regards good, they have learned many things.

With regard to the boys now at school, and without an exception, they have improved in many respects. They have been more punctual in their attendance, cleanlier in their persons, quieter and less rude in their manners, more moral in their general conduct, and more respectful and devout at worship. Considering the wretchedness, filthiness, drunkenness, irregularity, and immorality, above which they are rising, and for which they are acquiring a dislike, they have, by God's blessing, made some progress. Once it was a hard matter to gain their attention, now they will listen to any subject, and when their minds are turned to the works of Christ and his disciples, as recorded in the gospels, they are deeply interested. And this is my hope. For, if God's truth, stored up in the memory and implanted in the heart, does not do something for them, after all, even in this world, they are likely to remain wretched and depraved.

CASES.

No. 1 is the son of Roman Catholic parents of the lowest grade. I found him at school when I became teacher. I soon discovered that he was a rude, swearing, bully of a boy, though but eight years of age. The second day I came to school he quarrelled with another boy,

7

and threw him from the top to the bottom of the stairs. The next day he set off on a stroll. During several months he repeatedly left school, and could not be brought back but by force. His mother whipped him both at home and in school, but for every day that he was at school, he was two days absent, and in bad company. About eight months ago, after one of his strolls, which lasted for several days, he got up from the chimney corner, where he had lain all night, and at three o'clock in the morning called on another boy to get up and come to school. Since then he has not been once absent without a just reason.

No. 2 has no father. His mother is a low woman, and wretchedly poor. For her three children she has a small allowance from the parish, which, with what she earns by teasing oakum, is her means of support. Since the death of her husband she has been leading a grossly immoral life. The boy has been neglected from his birth, but, since the death of the father, who was a great drunkard, he became worse and worse. The mother sent him and a younger brother, also at school, to collect rags, bones, cinders, &c., but the former, who is an active boy, had no relish for this filthy burrowing employment, and, to mend the matter as he thought, joined a band of thieves. On following his new calling he was taken up and put in prison. After leaving prison he betook himself to his old work, and marked out the boys of the Ragged School as his prey, and again and again robbed them of the bread which several of them had been in the habit of saving for their brothers or sisters at home. Coming to the knowledge of this, I sent for him and offered to take him into the school, but, fearing the worst, he refused, and replied that I only wanted to beat him. Since then he came of his own accord, and has now been four months with us. The first week he was at school he mastered the alphabet, and continues to make progress; he still requires considerable management, but will work at anything, or do anything he is asked. He is punctual in his attendance, has given over swearing in school, and exhibits little of the bullying character which once attached to him. Out of school he has left his old companions, and keeps seasonable hours at night.

Master's notes.

The 'industry' emphasis in the school was growing. Rules were laid down in October 1849 which began: 'The object of the Society [i.e. the benevolent society which largely constituted the school's governing board] shall be to provide a Christian education for that neglected class of boys whose circumstances preclude their attendance at an ordinary school; to inure them to habits of industry, by regular employment; to remove the temptation to neglect school on the plea of searching for subsistence, by supplying them with an allowance of food daily.' This is a somewhat wider remit than the one proposed two years earlier. No mention of girls is made in these rules, despite the girls' school having been open for a year; this is because the girls' school was now producing its own reports.

These new 1849 rules stipulated that only one boy per family might attend the Ragged School for meals as well as lessons, although in certain cases one other could attend for lessons only. I imagine the thinking behind this was to prevent large families having their whole brood fed by the school whilst other families had no chance for even one child to benefit. But the jealousy and machinations of the 'unchosen' children in large families can be imagined. The rules also stated that prospective pupils be between eight and fourteen years old and have been resident in Newcastle for the previous twelve months.

The first Annual Report of the Girls' School, written by the schoolmistress, gives much more detail than the boys' counterpart. The pupils are described. Of a total of forty only twelve had both parents living. One girl was 'the child of a female convict, now transported'. A few children had left since starting the school but none had been expelled, the chief reason for leaving being 'family moving house'.

The girls' teacher, unnamed in the report because she wrote it, was a young woman from Glasgow. Like her deceased compatriot Mr Murray she seems to have been both successful and popular. She reports that Religious Instruction appealed most to the girls, especially certain passages from the Bible. They would spontaneously exclaim: 'that is beautiful!' and 'read that again!' Even a girl with a violent and uncontrollable temper eventually softened under the influence of the Bible readings. Or so says the young teacher, and I am inclined to believe her. Whatever may be said against religion, no one can deny its power to inspire hope and the vision of a wider reality into a wretched life.

It is significant, and says a great deal about the dedication of this young teacher, that no girl had been expelled. These were unbelievably difficult girls to teach. The teacher herself reports that 'their insubordination was very great, and some cases of actual rebellion took place'. One girl 'contemptuously absented herself for some days but expressed a wish to be readmitted.'. Looking beyond the teacher's natural understatement (she being a Victorian Scotswoman) and her passionate wish for the school and her teaching to be a success, we can form an idea of the mayhem that must have ruled from time to time. As to the girl who asked to be readmitted, one wonders whether her repentance was sharpened by thoughts of the hot meat stew that by this time had replaced bread and cheese at lunchtime.

One pathetic little pupil is described: 'aged nine, with no mother and a drunken father.' This little girl was often found late in the evening standing alone on the quayside. When asked why, she said she liked 'to catch the light' rather than 'remain at home alone in the dark'.

Quayside 1880. 'Catching the light' at dusk.

Another child living alone with a drunken father took a friend from school home with her to try to clean the room she and her father shared. The father, returning drunk, threw them both out, saying when he wanted help he would ask for it.

Such cases must have made the Governors realize how urgent was the need for full board and lodging for some children. By this same time, late 1849, the food had changed. Porridge was now given for breakfast, and soup with bread for lunch. The 'soup' was a meat stew cooked on the premises. The teacher's wife was responsible for buying ingredients and, one suspects, for much else besides. None of the reports mentions anyone employed to cook or serve meals. It is possible that the girl pupils did this, under the supervision of a trained cook. They certainly did later on, when the school was Industrial as well as Ragged. Another possibility is that in those early years the teacher's wife cooked and served the meals herself. Contemporary advertisements for schoolmasters invariably asked for married men whose wives would oversee the children's physical welfare. The wives of course received no wages: they were considered 'covered' by their husbands' salaries.

Notes

1.   MacKenzie, E. *op.cit.* (1827) p.11.
2.   From *Kelly's Trades Directory* for Newcastle upon Tyne 1850, under the heading 'Schools'. This publication is valuable in providing the kind of information we nowadays get from the Yellow Pages. However, its complete accuracy cannot be guaranteed: in other contexts I have found it mistaken in small details. It does, though, give a rough general picture of the number of schools in operation.
3.   'Board' here means the independent charitable board which had established the school. Not to be confused with the Government's School Boards in the latter part of the century.
4.   Watson, R.S. *op.cit.* p.10-11.
5.   The diet at this and other schools will be looked at in detail later.
6.   It is clear that the Government, even though not financially supporting the school in any way, intended, via the Council of Education, to ensure that basic standards were maintained. This was the same relationship that it (the Government) had with schools in factories.

4

The Schools Become 'Industrial'
as Well as 'Ragged'

In the early part of 1850 the shoemaker left the boys' school and was replaced by a tailor. Shoemaking had not made a profit, the costs having proved greater than any gains. Nor was tailoring expected to do any better commercially, but at least the boys would be able to wear the clothes they made. Already we see the trimming of high hopes to hard reality. Local newspapers of the time carry advertisements for clothes tailored by the school, and we can be fairly sure these advertisements did not have to be paid for. Even so, and even with occasional orders, the tailoring never paid its way for long. The work was of a high standard – everyone agreed on this – but the school could not afford to sell its wares cheaply. Commercial firms could.

The Boys' School report for January 1851 stresses the need for more subscriptions. The public was very ready to donate gifts in kind, especially, for some reason, cheese, but less ready to increase financial donations either in numbers or amount given. This was the first of the increasingly anxious appeals for money that marked most of the schools' history.

Proposals in this report show that the idea of the schools being at least partly 'Industrial' was taking hold. It was suggested that a practice current in Aberdeen could be applied to Newcastle. In Aberdeen, vagrant children rounded up by the police and delivered to that city's Industrial School rather than being put in prison had their cost of upkeep partly met by the prison service. After all, had the children gone to prison they would have had to be fed and lodged there. (This shows, in passing, that the Aberdeen Industrial School, which had started as a day school, now boarded at least some pupils.) The governors of the Newcastle Ragged Schools must have found the idea of regular Government funding very attractive, even if they had to lay out capital converting to boarding schools. Another practice from Scotland was discussed: the Edinburgh Industrial School had successfully appealed to citizens to sponsor individual boys, i.e. pay for their keep, for the whole of their school career. This could only work in a school that enforced attendance. Industrial Schools could do this, Ragged Schools could not.

The need for funds was becoming overriding. Whilst some boys worked in the tailoring shop for three hours daily, others were employed on picking oakum, turn and turn about. 'Picking oakum' meant unravelling ropes so that their fibres could be reused if fit and if not, thrown away. The report notes regretfully that that oakum-picking is 'not exactly what the Committee prefers for [the pupils], yet [it] yields some assistance to the funds.'

The main news from the Girls' School for this year is that the young mistress suffered a long illness in 1850 but was recovered by January 1851. Nothing is said about who did the teaching whilst she was ill.

Between 1851 and 1852 forty-six boys left their school, and the report of 1852 gives an analysis of them. Twelve had found employment, five had gone on to higher schools (this was a real achievement for a Ragged School child), three had gone into the workhouse (perhaps having become total orphans), seven had left the town, and one had died in a traffic accident, having been run over by a cart. Of the remaining eighteen, five had returned to begging, and thirteen had simply left, being 'unable to bear the discipline of the school'. Many of these thirteen had received teaching only, i.e. no food. They were brothers of boys enjoying the school's full provision. Since the school had no powers to enforce attendance it did well to hold on to so many pupils.

It was decided to lengthen the school day to 7 p.m. to keep the children off the streets as long as possible. Mention is made, quite casually, of six beds having been provided on the premises, showing that some children were already being boarded although the school was still only a Ragged School. Some Ragged Schools did board pupils from the beginning; most did not. In 1853 the Girls' School opened a second dormitory.

The lack of money led to an ominous decision to 'simplify' the meals provided 'in line with other schools' whilst still keeping them nutritious. Butchers' bills show that the cheapest meat was bought for the children's midday stew, and better meat for the staff. School governors had to be careful about such things. If the general public thought that lawless children in Ragged or Industrial Schools or in Reformatories were being fed more generously than the children of poor working men there would be an outcry and financial support would be withdrawn. According to medical officers' reports the children's health remained good even after the 'simplifying' of the meals, but over the years it deteriorated in one glaring respect. We will examine the diet in detail later.

Public kindness towards the schools was marked, and so was criticism of this kindness. From the beginning charitable individuals had supplied treats for the children, and in some years they laid on Christmas and New Year dinners for the children and their parents, showing an almost modern awareness that children can love even bad parents and want to be with them. Another treat was days out at Tynemouth, transport provided free, which became more and more frequent. This provoked criticism in the press and elsewhere. The complaint again was that 'charity' children were having better lives than the children of the hard-working poor. Poor parents might be tempted to get a child 'committed' both for its own sake and for their own.

The schools were criticised on other grounds. The illustrious Earl Grey advised that more of the school day should be spent in manual labour and less in book-learning. The governors could not ignore such a critic and so proposed buying a piece of land from the Borough Council and building proper workshops on it.

Appeals for donations of clean old clothes continued even after the tailoring shop was up and running. In fact it was unrealistic to expect twenty or so novice boys (i.e. those older ones who did the tailoring) to produce enough wearable clothes for the whole school and to keep replacing them as they wore out. Of course it is possible that some or all of the clothes produced were put out for sale to help with funds. The low-grade work of oakum-picking had come to an end and been replaced by the making of paper bags. But there was not much public demand for these; besides, the workhouse made them too.

Over and above other deficiencies loomed the need for more subscriptions, that is, guaranteed fixed annual donations. The number of these did rise, as did the number of single donations, but not

The school day was lengthened to keep children off the streets.

enough to ensure a firm financial foundation. Becoming a registered Industrial School would bring in a Government grant of £13 per pupil per annum for children sent there by magistrate's order.

For some years the idea of larger, purpose-built premises had been mooted and by 1854 had become a decision. The schools would be rebuilt and renamed. The fund-raising that this entailed and the school that resulted were described by R.S. Watson, Chairman of the schools' Board of Governors, in his 1867 pamphlet:

'A plot of ground, near the New Road, was granted [by the Town Council] at an annual rental of eight pounds, which was increased to ten pounds on more ground being found necessary. The Corporation afterwards enfranchised the property upon very liberal terms.[1] The building fund was largely subscribed to; the ladies of the town and neighbourhood raised by a bazaar the handsome sum of fifteen hundred and ten pounds; and the Privy Council gave material assistance, so that in one way or another ample means were forthcoming.

[T]he new Schools were formally opened upon the 24th of January 1855. The arrangements made for the industrial training of the children soon proved insufficient, and in 1857 the Corporation made a further grant of land, upon which workshops and dormitories for the boys were built. [A]t present fifty boys and thirty-three girls live upon the premises. It is now in contemplation to increase the dormitory accommodation so as to lodge ninety boys and forty-five girls, and the plans for the extension have been approved by the Home Secretary. The ground is nearly square, and contains about two thousand, two hundred and sixty-eight square yards. The buildings surround three sides of it. On the north side is the master's house, and adjoining it on the ground floor, a small tailors' work room, two workshops where mat making and sack making are carried on, store-rooms &c. On the upper floor are two dormitories for the boys, of the same size as the workshops, and divided by a small bedroom for the warden. The west side of the ground is open to the road. On the east side are the sitting-room for the

City Road, formerly New Road. This shows the Keelman's Hospital, further west than the site of the new school.

certified boys [i.e. those committed by magistrates and therefore boarders], the necessary offices [i.e. WCs], and a large playshed. A playground for the boys, one hundred and thirty feet by one hundred and twenty-four feet divides their workshops and dormitories from the other school buildings, and in this playground there is a full-rigged mast and spars which are a source of infinite enjoyment.

As you go from east to west you pass through a large wash-house fitted up with all modern conveniences, kitchens, pantries, and store-rooms, bath-rooms, committee-room, and then enter a dining-hall, which is sixty feet long by thirty feet wide, and sixteen feet high to the bottom of an open roof. Here all the scholars, boys and girls, of every class take their meals together; and in this room the annual examination, before the friends of the institution, is held. There are few sights pleasanter than it affords when it is well-filled with the children full of eager expectation for their annual Christmas dinner. Opening out of it on the west are the boys' and girls' school-rooms, whilst the girls' playground and shed lie behind to the south. If the place were to be rebuilt the girls would be allowed much more room to play in, for at their time of life there does not appear to be much difference between the sexes in their capacity for the enjoyment of active physical exercise. There is a good printing-room attached to the building on the north side of the dining-hall, where the scholars keep two presses in constant work, and the execution of this pamphlet, which has been printed there, shows that they understand their business.

Upstairs are the matron's room, and the house girls' sitting-room, dormitories, and sick-room. This part of the building is three stories high. It is kept clean by the girls, who also do the whole of the cooking, washing, and mending, for the entire establishment.

So much for the buildings: and now a word as to what is done with the children. The morning of each day is devoted to instruction in the elements of an ordinary plain education, and, during the afternoon, sewing, and the other industrial occupations, already alluded to, are carried on. [A footnote here says: The fact that as many as 300 sacks are sometimes made in a single afternoon, and that more than 10,000 have been made since the beginning of the year, shows that the work done is honest hard work, and no play.] In the evenings when the certified scholars are gathered in their sitting rooms they have different games which they play at, or they are read to by the officer who has charge of them. Go when you will in school-hours, work-time, or play-time, and you will rejoice to see so many happy children; and you will imagine that in the thin worn old faces growing child-like and plump and cheerful, you can trace the longer or shorter period which each has spent in this good resting place.

In 1859 the School was certified under the Industrial Schools Act[2] and the whole of the children at present in residence [i.e. boarders] (fifty boys and thirty-three girls) have been committed by the magistrates. There are also twenty-eight boys and thirty girls upon the food list [i.e. receiving full Ragged School benefits], and there are altogether upon the School Roll one hundred and forty-six boys and one hundred and fifteen girls, who are Ragged School scholars. [It is not clear whether these numbers include or exclude the 'food list' scholars]. There is no distinction whatever made in teaching or otherwise between the certified and uncertified children, excepting that the latter return home in the evening. All idea of prison or confinement is carefully excluded, and a stranger would find it at first difficult to tell which children had been committed to school and which came because their parents sent them.

The Schools are managed by a committee of sixteen gentlemen – seven of whom are trustees in whom the School premises are vested – and by a ladies' committee, upon which, of course, much of the active personal care devolves.'

Mr Watson does not mention that the new school was designed by the renowned John Dobson who had been responsible for so much of the architectural renewal of Newcastle.

We can see from the pupil numbers given that the school remained more 'Ragged' than 'Industrial': eighty-three children committed by magistrates (qualifying it as 'Industrial') as against 261 children attending voluntarily, some receiving meals, some not, qualifying the school as 'Ragged'. Moreover these figures refer to 1867, the year the pamphlet was written. The Annual Report for 1862 notes that of fifty-four new boys admitted in the past year, only five had been committed on a magistrate's order, i.e. about 10 per cent. But the same report gives a total figure of boarding pupils of thirty-one, the whole school population then being 112. This is much more than 10 per cent. So, either a higher proportion of previous years' intakes had been on magistrates' orders, or else some pupils boarded who were not 'committed'. The same year's report (1862) states that thirty-five boys had left, half of them to start work; of the other half all but seven had moved to other schools. Four had left 'without reason', two had been admitted to the workhouse (perhaps orphaned) and one had 'absconded'. In a completely Industrial School absconding would have been a serious matter resulting in either lengthening of the boy's 'sentence' at the school or transfer to a Reformatory. But Ragged School pupils were under no such compulsion. The Newcastle Schools were a mixture of the two as we have seen: they started as Ragged and then adapted themselves to qualify as 'Industrial' as well, and continued to take both types of pupil.

The new Newcastle Ragged and Industrial School.

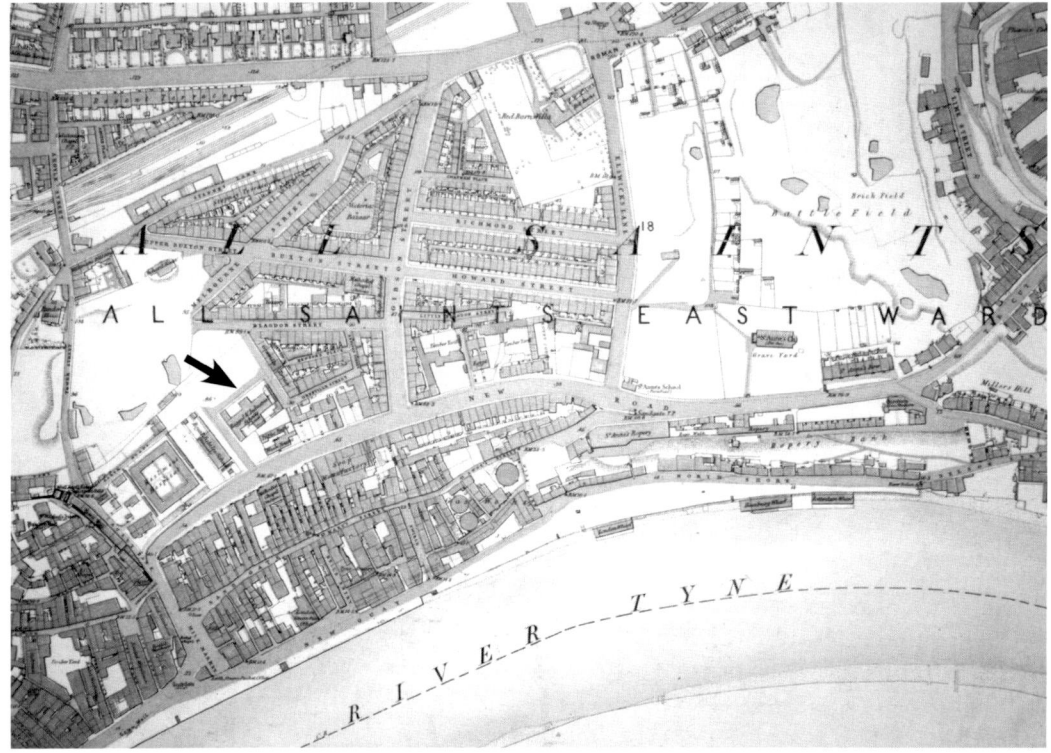

Map of part of Newcastle showing the site of the new school.

Notes

1. The New Road later became City Road and the 'piece of land' mentioned was on Jubilee Road. The 'Jubilee' in the name does not of course refer to Queen Victoria but to the Jubilee of George III. There had been a 'Royal Jubilee School' – an ordinary private middle-class school there for some time.
2. This was the second Industrial Schools Act (21 Victoria c.48) and covered existing schools which had modified themselves to qualify as 'Industrial'. The first Act (20 Victoria) referred to schools set up as 'Industrial' from the outset.

5

Continuities and Change, Successes and Failures

The Schools' Annual Report for 1862 notes that industry all over the country is depressed as a result of the American Civil War and the consequent loss of markets. It was useless therefore to expect the schools' workshops to show a profit. (This looks like a fig leaf as we have seen that previous years made no profit either). The boys were still tailoring and repairing clothes but, sadly, also back to oakum-picking, sack-making, hair-teasing and mat-making. Such activities were the basic employment of the workhouses too, and some of the prisons. There was a limit to how many sacks, mats and unpicked ropes a town could use, or even a country. A note of desperation sounds in the report's assertion that such lowly and unskilled work nevertheless has value in breaking children's street habits and instilling the regularities of work. 'After all, we cannot be expected to teach trades.'

Donations and treats for the children continued throughout the hardship. Because the boys committed by magistrates and therefore accompanied by a Home Office grant were generally better clothed than the others, many benefactors sent clothes especially for those 'others'. Such philanthropy was criticised in essays, in Parliament, and in newspapers[1], yet the donations and treats continued. 1863 was a good year for the children. Between 3 July and 10 September they had three full-day and two half-day excursions, to Cullercoats, to Bamborough, to Warkworth Castle, and to Sir William Armstrong's new stately home at Cragside. Health remained good: the year saw only single cases of long illness in the infirmary: in other words, no epidemics. However as we shall see the children's health declined later in this decade due to deficiencies in the diet.

There was an exhibition in London of work done in all the Industrial Schools in the country. The Newcastle Schools sent samples of their work but the report does not say what. I imagine they were products of the printing press and tailoring shop; they could hardly have been unravelled rope and a sack.

For several years the Girls' School made steady undramatic progress with little to report. This does not mean, though, that all was well: 1864 saw a short-lived staffing crisis. It should be remembered that at that time any woman who married had to give up her job: therefore turnover among women staff would naturally be higher than among men. Other facts were less easily explained. The report of 1866 notes that girls had more long-term sickness than boys. Moreover, their lives seemed less happy. The 'needlework' they did was chiefly mending the boys' shirts and socks. We have seen from the Watson pamphlet that the girls did all the cooking,

Children's street habits had to be broken.

A children's treat organised by philanthropists. This one was at a later date.

cleaning and mending for the entire establishment, and also that their playground was too small. The much-lauded printing press was never used to teach printing to a girl. Whereas the boys were in theory at least being taught skills that could prepare them for a variety of work, the girls were all quite openly being trained to domestic service and nothing else. Of course the same was true for 90 per cent of women at the time. It could be counter-argued however that these were the years when women in general began to chafe at the narrowness of their lives. Mary Carpenter said that girls in her Ragged School were harder to deal with than boys, and it was well known that many disturbances in the workhouses consisted of windows being smashed by girls. We have seen the remarkable success attained by many of the boys who left the schools; the results for were less good. There was one star who became headmistress of a girls' school in Halifax, and plenty who obtained good domestic jobs. But the 1865 report, using Victorian euphemism, notes that '[some girls], when removed from the wholesome influences of their school life [have experienced] difficulty'. There is no need to spell out what was meant. The lives of the girls at the Newcastle Schools were the subject of a stinging criticism meted out by a female Home Office Inspector some decades later.

Industrial Schools were inspected by the Home Office twice yearly, one visit announced, the other unannounced. In 1865 the Inspector judged the Newcastle Schools favourably, allotting both to the 'first rank of schools of this class'. He had one criticism which was the exact opposite of Earl Grey's: the industrial training, thought the Inspector, was good, but the academic standards in the three 'R's were low, although that was partly to be expected 'given the class of children attending'. The schools should devote more time to the three 'R's (and presumably less to manual skills). Berated on the one hand for giving too much book-learning (Earl Grey) and on the other for not enough (HM Inspector), the schools must have been doing something right because that year all the 'old boys' were doing well and none were in prison.

There were still many neglected little girls on the streets.

The 1866 report carried the sickening news that the printing, like the tailoring and shoemaking, had failed to make any money. From this year on the pleas for subscriptions and donations became more and more desperate. The Girls' School report made the first mention of 'kitchen girls', saying: 'There are thirty-eight girls boarded and lodged in the house. Out of these, twelve girls are selected for the house work [by what criteria, one wonders?] cleaning, cooking, washing etc who are thus trained under the matron to perform the duties of domestic servants.' A footnote added 'These girls when not engaged in their domestic duties are sent into the School to continue their education, and two evenings a week attend the class of the elder scholars.' Were these girls committed by magistrates or boarded under some other arrangement? Why were they treated differently from the other twenty-six girl boarders? I have scanned the reports for answers to these questions without finding any.

1867's report is interesting because of an elliptical reference to discipline. 'Discipline is strictly maintained whilst nothing of a prison character is introduced'. One senses a debate not reported here, with the schools under attack perhaps from two opposing viewpoints. Perhaps this was part of the ongoing 'easier life for the lawless than the law-abiding' accusation.

There were plans to enlarge the schools, particularly to build proper workshops for the boys, but far from being able to expand, their continuing existence was threatened unless more money could be found. The Girls' School in a separate report echoed the lack of money; in particular there were no wearable clothes for the Day pupils, i.e. those not committed on magistrate's order. Gifts in kind were still coming in and one wonders why no cloth merchant made a gift of some bolts of material so that the girls could make clothes for themselves. There is a sense that the girls' school was not doing well. There had been many changes of staff and some serious illness among the children. One little invalid girl who had appeared to be recovering had died.

In 1868 the planned extensions went ahead: sponsors had finally put up the money. Besides workshops, an extra dormitory was built and a house for a superintending master. The site was close to the school itself. However, there was an outbreak of scarlet fever at the boys' school as a result of which all the pupils were moved to Forster Street Hospital. Once there they all recovered. Forster Street was an early Isolation Hospital; its success in saving the children and preventing the spread of infection proved a strong argument in favour of such hospitals.

Testimonials from 'old boys' are again included in this report but they raise one's suspicions, being almost identical with those from an earlier year. One cannot help wondering whether the same ones had been reprinted with the aim of making the school attractive to possible benefactors.

A second Government inspection had produced a favourable report on the improved academic standards following the enlargement of the premises. But the financial situation had become so bad that the board had applied to the Corporation for an additional annual contribution for each 'committed' child (to boost the £13 p.a. from the Home Office) and to the Board of Poor Law Guardians for a contribution for each uncommitted child whose parents were on Parish Relief. Both of these bodies were considering the proposals.

The 22nd Annual Report, for 1869, had a brilliant success to record! The lady managers of the Girls' School had organised a bazaar which had earned almost £2,000 (about £100,000 in today's money). The schools, for the first time, were out of debt! The report however did not slacken the pressure on the burghers of Newcastle, pointing out that the problem of regular income remained. Newcastle Corporation had turned down the application for further grants for 'committed' pupils but increased its own annual subscription to sixty guineas. The Poor Law Guardians however had granted the request for grants for children of parents on Parish Relief.

The Girls' School report for this year was again slightly disquieting. The girls' manual work was described as something to be proud of: '[They] keep [the buildings] scrupulously clean, and do all the washing, cooking, mending &c., both for boys and girls.' But one cannot help feeling their lives were constricted and dull. They were taught the three 'R's but more haphazardly than the boys, a detail among many severely criticised some years later by a female Inspector. Also disturbing is the fact that girls who had left and gone into service (the only career for the great majority) were now required to pay back £1 from their first quarter's wages to the school. Certainly the school needed all the pounds it could get, but why was not the same requirement made of the boys? The Girls' report, perhaps more honest than the Boys', admitted again that 'Of those who have left the school, it cannot be said that all have turned out well'. Turning out well was important: there was a general expectation that such schools should show a return for expenditure in the form of pupils turning out well. Reading the Schools' Annual Reports we must never forget that the writers would be tempted to paint the rosiest picture (except, as we have seen, some of the honest women teachers). If the burghers reading the reports felt the schools were making no difference to crime and poverty they would withdraw their funding. But there would be an additional motive for showing things in the best light, namely the board's own wish to have its judgement vindicated and see the project succeed. Utopian hopes are not easily given up.

The old Fever Hospital's House of Recovery.

By the late 1860s political ideas which had originated in other parts of public life began to influence education. Proudhon in France and Marx and Engels in England formulated versions of socialism which never took vigorous root in England, but the country's own Radicals had a profound effect. According to Brian Simon in *History of Education 1780-1870,* 'The philosophical radicals were among the first to put forward the idea of universal education. Indeed they worked actively in the cause of the enlightenment of the masses on rational and unsectarian lines and advocated compulsory elementary education for all.'[2] The Radicals wanted a vastly extended franchise so that Government could never again be cornered by the aristocracy and gentry. This was a very different motive from that of the Christian Protestants who believed that every soul must make the most of its talents and bring them to God, even though the Church's actual schooling had long since ceased to live up to such noble ideals. Simon argues that the working class saw through the Radicals' apparent benevolence to their true motive which was the strengthening of the middle class against the aristocracy and the Church. The Deist Tom Paine had said 'A Nation under a well-regulated Government should permit none to remain uninstructed. It is monarchical and aristocratical Government only that requires ignorance for its support'.[3] As we have seen, plenty of working people could read Paine's works and plenty did. For example 'The Sheffield Constitutional Society,' which is said to have numbered 2,000 well-behaved men, most of them of the lower sort of workmen, met regularly for class discussion, reprinted *The Rights of Man* at the low price of 6d per copy and formed branches in neighbouring districts in order 'to extend useful knowledge from town to village, and from village to town, until the whole nation be sufficiently enlightened'.[4] It could be argued that, just as the Radicals proposed mass education to further their own ends, the working classes, through Combinations and powerful spokesmen, used Radical-inspired initiatives for theirs. By the late 1860s universal elementary education was an idea whose time had come: not yet spoken of as a 'right' but with as much force as if it were. But if education for every child was the aim its provision should be standardised and not left to the haphazardness of private boards of governors. This at least was the Benthamite argument. Certainly most educational establishments were already inspected by the Council of Education, but, it was argued, it would be better to have the whole business centralised: provided and managed by the Government and paid for out of general taxation. The subject was debated passionately and at length in Parliament and resulted in the Elementary Education Act of 1870.

The Newcastle Schools' Annual Report for 1870 noted the Parliamentary debates and resulting Act without any comment. The same lack of comment had characterised a mention in the 1869 Annual Report of a debate in Parliament on the idea of a national, i.e. Governmental solution to the ills of vice and crime. Such a solution would require national resources, i.e. taxation. Of course a school's Annual Reports are not the place for long discussions of such subjects but it is surprising to see matters so central to the Industrial Schools reported so laconically. The governors seem to have given far more attention to immediate, day-to-day news.

Donations of second-hand clothes had stopped because people were sending everything to the newly-formed Red Cross for victims of the Franco-Prussian war. It seems to have been a year of trouble for both the boys' and the girls' schools. No details were given, but the figures told the story. Of the fifty-seven boys who had left during the year, eighteen (almost a third) had been discharged for non-attendance or 'unsuitableness'. One would dearly like to have this 'unsuitableness' explained. Was it indiscipline, or something worse? Running pickpocketing

Another view of the New Road school buildings.

Outside Central Station. Excursions on newly opened railway lines were popular.

gangs from the school? After all most of the pupils were day-attenders with full access to the outside world. The Girls' School figures were similarly disquieting. Of seventy-six who left in the year, twenty-eight (again almost a third) 'left without reason'; in addition twelve were 'dismissed'. The report did not say why. All in all, over half of the girls who left did so for bad reasons. One can only speculate why the schools should be calm and successful one year and stressed and disturbed the next. They were housed in the new buildings so physical hardship could not have been to blame. To compound the mystery the Government Inspector's report for 1870 was again excellent! One explanation suggests itself. It is possible that the schools deliberately expelled the most troublesome pupils in order to get a good Government report. They could not of course expel 'committed' pupils without Home Office permission but with the Ragged school pupils they could do as they wished.

Notes

1. The Malthusian idea was abroad that easing the lot of the poor increased their numbers, thus there was never any reduction in poverty.
2. *Op. cit.* (1960) p.126.
3. Paine, Tom: *The Rights of Man.* Everyman Edition (1961) p.256.
4. Bamford, Samuel: *Early Days* (ed. Henry Dunckley 1893) p.53-4. Quoted in Simon, Brian, *op. cit.* p.182.

6

Day-to-Day Life
in the Schools

Up to 1870 the Schools' Annual Reports were published anonymously, that is, without any individual officer of the board mentioned as author or compiler. But from 1870 they were issued as 'Superintendent's Reports'. The Superintendent was appointed by the schools' own governing board but had to be made known to the Home Office Inspectors. The Superintendent's reports take the form of monthly minuted meetings following a Government recommendation to all boards of Industrial Schools. From these Minutes I have taken the material for this and subsequent chapters.

In 1870 the Superintendent revealed that several children had suffered from scurvy in the preceding year, attributed by 'one of our Surgeons' to a 'lack of vegetable food'. The deficiency had since been remedied and the children were all now well. There had been one mild case of smallpox, as a result of which all the children had been vaccinated, some of them for the second time.

In this year a 'General Dietary Table' for the schools was published, but it is not clear whether these were the meals before or after the 'vegetable food' was added.

Breakfast: Sunday, Tuesday, Friday: 1 pint coffee with sugar and milk. 4 or 6 ounces of bread, according to age. Monday, Wednesday, Thursday, Saturday: 1 pint of porridge with milk.

Dinner: Monday: 1 pint broth, 3 ounces meat, 4 or 6 ounces bread (again by age). Tuesday, Thursday, Saturday: 1 pint pea soup, 3 ounces meat, 4 or 6 ounces bread. Friday: 1 pint broth, 3 ounces bread, 4 or 6 ounces suet pudding and treacle. Sunday: 1 pint potato stew, 3 ounces meat, 4 or 6 ounces bread.

Tea: ½ pint milk and 4 or 6 ounces bread daily except Sunday. Sunday 1 pint tea or coffee.

Supper: bread and treacle: 5 ounces to big boys, 3 ounces to girls and little boys.

The nutritional imbalance of this diet seems shocking, but it is well to remember that it reflected the general food of the poor at the time. The cause of scurvy had been identified early in the century but it took generations to change eating habits. Not even the upper classes thought fruits and vegetables essential; indeed Bertrand Russell in his autobiography tells how as a child he was denied an orange for dessert even though all the adults were having them, because fruit was thought bad for children! In the nineteenth century bread was the staple food of the poor, but a lot of cooked food was sold by street traders in poor districts. According to Henry Mayhew there were 'hot-eels, pickled whelks, oysters, sheeps' trotters, fried fish, ham sandwiches, hot green peas, kidney puddings, boiled meat puddings, beef, mutton, kidney, and eel pies, and baked potatoes. In each of these provisions the street-poor find a mid-day or midnight meal'.[1] Small mention of vegetables there although fruit tarts and pies were also sold.

Even in the country poor peoples' diets were monotonous and centred around bread. Flora Thompson in *Lark Rise to Candleford* mentions that farm labourers breakfasted on bread spread with lard and often lunched on the same. Lucky ones had a piece of cold bacon added. Tea was drunk without milk as the labourers owned no cows. But country children were usually healthy, probably because they gathered their own vegetables in stealth. According to Flora Thompson, on their way to school these children would 'creep through the bars of the padlocked field gates for turnips or for handfuls of green pea shucks, or ears of wheat. In spring they ate the young green from the hawthorn hedges and sorrel leaves from the wayside and in autumn there was an abundance of haws and blackberries and sloes and apples for them to feast upon'. City children had no such plenty to call on, whatever their social class.

So although the Newcastle Schools' diet was poor by modern standards it was reasonable for its time. Certainly amounts of food were adequate and there was enough first-class protein. But the lack of fruits and vegetables is marked, and it is no mystery to us why they had scurvy. One would like to know exactly how the deficiency was made up, i.e. what was added to the meals and how long it took for the children to become well again. The brisk, almost offhand way the matter is treated in the Superintendent's Report suggests the hushing-up of a scandal. Or perhaps once again simply the unwillingness of the school's patrons, like people in general, to admit any fault in their beloved project.

As well as the table of diet the schools published a 'General Time Table' in 1870.

6-8.30 a.m. Rise, beds made, house and kitchen work for girls, cleaning yards etc. for boys, washing and getting self ready.

8.30–9 a.m. Breakfast.

9-12 noon. Kitchen girls doing housework, the other dormitory girls in school with the boy children. One half of the boys in school, the other half at industrial work in workshops.

12-12.30 p.m. Dinner

12.30-1.30 p.m. Recreation and preparation.

1.30-5.00 p.m. School and work. Boys who worked in the morning now in school, and vice versa. All the dormitory [i.e. boarding] girls, including the kitchen girls, in school with the day children on Tuesdays, Wednesdays and Thursdays. On Mondays, Fridays and Saturdays the kitchen girls worked in the afternoon at the usual cooking, washing, scouring etc.

5.00 p.m. Tea

5-8.00 p.m. Boys' and girls' recreation, except for Tuesdays and Thursdays, when all the dormitory girls, including the kitchen girls, receiving instruction in the school from 5.30 until 7.30.

[8 p.m. presumably supper and bed. Not noted].

The work of each day began and closed with prayers and Bible readings. However, the children were not taught the Catechism, and this was deliberate policy. Education in general was wrenching itself free of the Church of England. Industrial Schools being, as we have seen, a somewhat utopian Enlightenment project[2], were not intended to be hamstrung by Anglican religious dogma. Of course Churches of any denomination could set up Industrial Schools of their own, such as the Roman Catholic St James' and St Elizabeth's in Newcastle and St George's in Liverpool, and the religious practices there would be very different from those of the Newcastle Ragged and Industrial Schools. Day children at these latter schools, the subject of this study, attended Sunday School if their parents wished it. As for church attendance on Sundays, where children's religious denomination were known arrangements were made to escort parties to the appropriate church. Otherwise there was no doctrinal compulsion to attend, although in practice children not attending any designated church were taken to a local Anglican one on Sunday mornings simply to have them under supervision! Thus do great arguments about freedom of belief come to rest on the ground of everyday life.

In the summer the children were taken en masse for days at the seaside, and later when the school had built its own seaside home, in groups for two weeks' holiday at a time.

Children at the seaside, late nineteenth century.

Not all children of working-class parents had two weeks' seaside holiday each year, so the children at the school had some comparative luxury in their lives.

It will be seen from the General Time Table that the 'kitchen girls' had more work and less leisure than other pupils. These girls were first mentioned in the 1866 Girls' school report, with a provoking lack of explanation about who they were and how they were selected.

A letter from one ex-pupil to his brother still at the school was printed in the report. The letter writer was in Lucknow, India [possibly with the Army] and urged his brother to study harder than he did himself and to follow the example of a third brother, George, who was now in 'a nice situation'. Commenting on this, the Superintendent explained: 'The brother George was also an old pupil of the school, and it is pleasant to record that though left fatherless and motherless he has managed by the exercise of his talent and ability to attain a highly respectable position in India. [He] has sent a gift of £20 to his sister who was also educated at [the] school and who married a few months ago a worthy mechanic and is now comfortably settled in a neighbouring village. This single family of orphans all doing well is but one instance of the benefit and blessing of these Schools.' This is a success story indeed, and one which could not take place today. For one thing England has a much reduced standing army now to provide careers for energetic boys. For another we can no longer 'export' poor but gifted people to make their way in the Empire. Chiefly of course there is no longer any Empire. The poor but gifted have to struggle along with the rich gifted and the rich ungifted-but-connected for such careers as are available here.

The report of 1871 stated that the Home Secretary, Mr Bruce, had proposed reducing the amount of Government grant to children committed on magistrate's order from £13 p.a. to £7.10 for those between ages six and ten and the over-fifteens. The reason for this was the huge strain on the Treasury made by existing grants, but the pretext was that children under ten were not capable of industrial training. In response, the Newcastle Schools proposed to admit in future only those committed children who were older than ten so as not to lose the higher grant. The report mentioned in passing that children admitted under the age of six got no Government grant whatever. It seems strange that under-sixes were at the school at all: the aims of the original Ragged School had been to educate 'about fifty boys aged six to fourteen', and later inclusion in the 'Industrial Schools' category certainly did not require children under six to be admitted as they were not liable for imprisonment anyway. But reports from other Industrial Schools did mention very young children being taken in from time to time, so perhaps it was common unofficial practice.

The Newcastle Boys' School had been asked to take some of the boys from the *Wellesley* Training Ship. It will be recalled that these ships were used by the Home Office as either Industrial Schools and Reformatories, having been started by the Marine Society in the eighteenth century. The School was considering the proposal. Presumably such boys would bring a Government grant with them.

Children were beginning to be sent to Industrial Schools by the new local authority School Boards, and their fees were paid out of the School Board allocation. The most usual reason for sending them was truancy. Rounding up truanting children became a job for both the police and the 'School Board Men'.

It seems the local Juvenile Prison Boards now had some influence and control over Industrial Schools as well as Reformatories which meant that the schools could draw funding from the Prison Service in certain cases. This could not have been a substantial provision or the schools would not have been in the permanent financial straits which they were in. In the Minutes of 1872 a request was received from London for the Newcastle Schools to accept some pupils,

Boys on the *Wellesley* Training Ship. The Newcastle School was asked to take some of them.

presumably because the London Industrial and Ragged Schools were full. London would pay all the costs. The Schools had agreed to take these pupils.

It was reported in 1873 that the workshops were finally making a profit. '£182 15s 0d is charged for workmasters and the master printer and the profit from Boys' and Girls' labour to cover this last year was £288 2s 1d. There were about 137 certified [committed] scholars last year and 181 day scholars, so that 7/9 of the profit is made by the certified scholars. Cost of maintenance of each certified scholar is about £14.7.3d per annum. But there is also a total annual expenditure of about £605 for the day scholars [i.e. about £3 10s 0d per child]. Our subscription list amounts to about £419. Interest on investments £133. Works Department £280, total £832. Our income last year [1872] exceeded our expenditure by about £400, but the expenditure will be greatly added to this year by increase of salaries, and the interest on investments will be lessened by our purchase of the new ground and other outlays.'

The reason for the increased income was then revealed. The schools had being doing 'contract' work for some time. The work was sent by firms to the schools to be done there; some though had asked for boys to be released daily to work at the factory. This was refused, which seems an enlightened decision. The boys concerned must have been younger than fourteen, otherwise apprenticeship schemes could have operated. Factory work would have interfered with their education, indeed with their whole routine, even though legislation was

Board School truants being rounded up.

in place to ensure that working children got some schooling. A resolution had been passed to accept no more hair for teasing. One applauds this decision too!

Throughout the 1870s and 1880s the Annual Reports are a mixture of domestic details and notes on the effects of Government policy. It is important to realise that day-to-day troubles and triumphs counted as largely as the policy effects; perhaps more so. This is always true in real life and this chapter aims to give a picture of the daily life of the schools. Accordingly, a list of typical triumphs and troubles follows. The next chapter will concentrate chiefly on the effects of Government policy.

Outbreaks of infectious illnesses plus the charges levied by the isolation hospital.

Evidence of an 'American Centrifugal Wringing Machine' in the school, showing that although the girls had to do the washing for the entire establishment they did not have to do everything by hand.

A proposal to heat the dormitories.

A proposal to buy a steam engine to drive a circular saw for woodcutting.

Prosecution of a married couple for assisting three girls to abscond. The girls themselves were punished by having their hair cut.

A proposal to take the children on a day trip to Saltburn on the newly-opened railway.

Accusation of indecent conduct against the boys' school Warden by two boys and an ex-boy. The Warden left speedily and no charges were pressed.

The boys' brass band was earning money giving concerts and had added reed instruments.

A suggestion that brown bread be served instead of white twice weekly. Sickly children to continue to be given 'tonic'.

Resolution that youngest boys should not start manual work until 7 a.m. (Masters started at 6.30)

Sick children taken to Cullercoats for sea and air bathing.

Children with incurable diseases to be discharged into the new Home for Incurables.

Most usual serious illnesses consumption (TB) and pneumonia. No child to be discharged from school until fit and well even if it is on a magistrate's order and has served the mandatory 'sentence'.

A cross-jack yard for the mast in the boys' playground given by Messrs. A.& R. Hopper, shipbuilders.

Assistant master's salary raised to 8s weekly.

Roman Catholic priest given permission to teach the RC children one hour weekly and have them accompanied to Mass on Sundays.

The Ladies' Committee had turned down an offer of 'flock' (sheep-shearing leftovers) for the girls' mattresses, preferring straw.

A bootmaker employed by the school dismissed for stealing workshop supplies.

Entry in the visitors' book objecting to coloured blankets on the children's beds.

Purchase of a knitting machine for the girls to make stockings.

Profits from boys' workshops in 1880: £96 19s 6d. from printing, £51 16s 7d from bootmaking and repairing, £174 2s 0d from ready-chopped firewood, £439 13s 8d from sack-making. Profit from total of girls' work: £76 7s 1d.

Fire in the school laundry.

Hiring of a permanent nurse.

Outbreak of diarrhoea throughout whole school, thought to have been caused by pease pudding.

Notes

1. This and following quotations on the subject of food are taken from Bentley, Nicolas: *The Victorian scene: a picture book of the period 1837-1901.*

2. In England at least. In Germany Protestantism with a belief in the edifying power of work already in place had less need of utopian visions for education.

7

Effects of Old and New Legislation

We have already seen that legislation on Industrial Schools and to a lesser extent on Ragged Schools was frequently altered over the years; after the 1870 Elementary Education Act both kinds of school found themselves in a new situation.

The Act was felt to have made many Ragged Schools unnecessary (though this was not its original intention) since many of the children they accepted could now go to the new Government Board Schools, provided some means could be found to pay any fees required. The new Board Schools were supposed to complement existing charitable schools, not replace them (at least that was the argument), and Ragged Schools continued to exist right up until the First World War, but their days were numbered, as some on both sides of the argument had foreseen. However, those same new Board Schools were experiencing a huge problem with truancy. This was dealt with by 'committing' the truants to a spell in an Industrial School. There were not enough existing Industrial Schools, so School Boards set about building Day Industrial Schools expressly for these truants.

The Newcastle School's Minutes for March 1877 cover a proposal to add a Day Industrial School function – and purpose-built premises – to its existing remit. The idea was to admit no more children of the 'Ragged School' category but fill the vacancies with Board School truants. So it would no longer be a Ragged and Industrial School but two kinds of Industrial School – Day and boarding – combined. Minutes of the previous year speak of possible 'extensions' to the school; it is likely that these were the proposed Day Industrial School. However, the Government refused certification and the idea was abandoned. The school could and did still accept as boarders children 'committed' for truanting, so long as the School Board 'make up with the Treasury allowance the total sum of 5s 6d per child, as for those sent under the Industrial Schools Act 1866. In other words, money was not to be lost by taking these children.

It will be recalled that any child who absconded from an Industrial School was liable to a final penalty of being placed in a Reformatory, provided he or she was over twelve. The Minutes record that this penalty had to be applied to one boy who had originally been sent to the school for truanting from a Board School.

A straw in the coming wind was shown in a request received from a London Reformatory for the Newcastle School to take some of their boys. It had to be refused as there were no free places. But the fact that it was made at all indicates that the boundaries between Industrial Schools and Reformatories were becoming fluid in practice if not yet in theory.

In the 1870s children began to be weighed and measured in accordance with a directive from the Anthropometric Committee of the British Association for the Advancement of Sciences. This may have been part of the new urge toward standardisation which had shown itself in the 1870 Elementary Education Act, or it may have had a more sinister motive in the new theory of the 'criminal type' which was gaining ground in some intellectual circles. This propounded that criminals and children likely to become criminals had distinctive physical characteristics. (This is no more than a suspicion on my part for which I have no evidence apart from the coincidence of dates.)

A letter had been received from the War Office 'asking if we wished our name put on the list of schools from which boys are selected for service in the Army or Navy'. The request was declined; one would have liked to have heard the arguments.

The Government had begun to criticise the manual work done in Industrial Schools. It was noted in the Newcastle School that the constructive work of printing and boot-making yielded profits which taken together were less than that produced by firewood-chopping, and that all three of these plus profit from the girls' work came to far less than the money made by sack-making. A later Government Report on Reformatories and Industrial Schools singled out for disapproval wood-chopping and similar non-constructive work in such schools.[1] It admitted, though, that the schools had to get money somehow and itself had no new suggestions as to how this could be done. These activities did make money and keep the schools going at a time when the Government itself was seeking to reduce its own grants to the schools, so its criticism seems impertinent. I would argue that this was an example of the *de haut en bas* attitude which does not bother itself with how principles work out in practice but leaves that to the servants, who can then be blamed if things go wrong. The fact remains that one way or another the schools were financially comfortable during these years.

This ease was not to last long: unfavourable signs were beginning to appear. The 1882 report noted that sensational stories had appeared in the press about bad conditions and harshness in Reformatories and Industrial Schools. None of the accusations was quoted, unfortunately; one would dearly like to have seen them. The writers had been careful not to run foul of libel laws by naming individual schools, and the Newcastle Schools usually had favourable annual Inspectors' Reports so there were no grounds for suspecting an attack upon them. Even so the newspaper stories must have been unnerving.

The latest Inspector's Reports had pronounced, worryingly, that the schools' scholastic levels were not up to those of other kinds of school, i.e. the new Board Schools. This had been attributed to (1) the children's 'dense ignorance' on admission, and (2) the fact that only half the day was spent on schooling. I should like to suggest another explanation: the new Board Schools, by accepting all categories of children except the criminal, the invalid and the insane, had unwittingly creamed off those neglected and destitute 'street children' who happened to be clever, in other words those who earlier would have been the Newcastle Schools' Ragged pupils. And since in their place the Newcastle Schools were accepting truants from those same Board Schools, i.e. children who would not settle to education, it would not be surprising that their examination results went down.

From 1883 to 1887 the Minutes are missing. However, later reports refer to a 'new building' which must have gone up during these years: this may well have been the 'swimming bath' which is referred to without comment in the 1893 report. We can presume the schools continued financially secure, due to the profits of the 'undesirable' work and the increased number of Government grants following the growing number of 'committed' children at the schools. These must have been the best years of the schools' life and it is provoking that we have no reports of them.

A Ragged School in 1846. This is an idealised version: most Ragged Schools had far less industrial training and the children were much wilder than those shown here.

Left: Ragged School pupils, 1910.

Opposite: Newcastle old gaol. More and more alternatives to gaol for child criminals were coming into existence.

Later reports refer to a seaside holiday home being part of the school's endowment: it may well have been built in these missing years. Industrial Schools and Reformatories were considered so successful that in 1895 the Gladstone Committee recommended the setting up of similar institutions for the sixteen to twenty-five age group, which eventually came into being as the Borstals.[2] But in that same year a very different Government report appeared, highly critical of the wholesale use of such institutions. The effects of this second report will be examined later.

Before either of these reports appeared a Government Act was passed in 1887 which, as things turned out, was one contributory cause of the eventual demise of Industrial Schools, at least as their founders had envisaged them. This 1887 Act established probation as a penalty for young criminal first offenders, so that it was no longer the case that for a child criminal to escape being sent to gaol he was usually put in some other kind of institution. We can see the Act as evidence of a new approach to juvenile crime: one that no longer believed residential institutions were the best way to rehabilitate first-time offenders of any age, including juveniles. According to W.R. Cornish and G. de N. Clark: 'The justices had long had power to discharge persons on recognisances to be of good behaviour; dedicated reformers, such as M.D. Hill, had encouraged experiments in supervised freedom as an alternative to a custodial sentence; legislation made it

possible to place offenders under the supervision of the police.' In a footnote we are told that the Probation of First Offenders Act, passed in 1887, was promoted by Sir Howard Vincent, the creator of Scotland Yard.[3]

If cynical, we can wonder whether this was thought an excellent way to deal with young offenders without having to pay for their upkeep in prisons or Industrial Schools and Reformatories.

The effects of the Probation Act would not be felt for some time however. The Government recommendation that most affected the Newcastle Schools in 1887 was that they separate into single-sex establishments. The Newcastle Schools' Board of Governors wrote an impassioned letter to the Home Secretary begging that the schools be left as they were, and pointing out that the two sexes did not mix except at mealtimes and even then they had separate tables. It was true that the girls had less playing space than the boys, but this could be remedied if the schools could move, as they wished to, to a more salubrious location and sell the present buildings. I suspect that Inspectors' criticisms about life in the girls' school, which were to culminate in the damning report of 1909, were already making themselves felt.

In the event the schools elected to comply with the new directive, first receiving an assurance that if and when they opened a separate school for girls, outside the town limits as recommended, Government grants for the girls would still go into the combined schools' coffers. By 1892 a possible site was being considered at Forest Hall, Benton, and the schools' board of governors wondered whether the National School Board might agree to contribute to the cost of a building. This project came to nothing, for reasons that will become clear.

By 1893 an agreement had been reached with the Home Office that parents of 'committed' children could remove them permanently before the expiry of their sentence. Each case would be considered individually and Home Office permission would be required.

In 1889, at Government examinations, 99 per cent of boys passed and 96 per cent of girls. It seems the Inspectors' earlier criticism of the schools' scholastic standards had been heeded. The Home Office Inspector for 1894 noted 'clear indications of careful and considerate treatment of the children as well as good exam results'. The girls' school however was damned with faint praise: 'I was glad to find much improvement and greater intelligence than I did last year.' The 1895 Inspector pronounced the discipline to be 'firm, but at the same time kindly, discriminating, and most encouraging. The success of the School depends upon the rational and humane development of the natural goodness and virtue each child has inherited, coupled with the correction and repression of all that is base, dishonest, degrading, and mean'. But he criticised the 'lavatories' (almost certainly washrooms) as in need of improvement.

These favourable words contrast with an 1895-6 report of a Committee on Reformatory and Industrial Schools which, according to Cornish and de N. Clark 'was heavily critical of the majority of these establishments, for their harsh and discouraging regimen. A minority of the Committee, moreover, denounced the asylum theory, adopted by some magistrates and school authorities, which led to children being sent to the schools whenever they would be better off and not only when the step was necessary to protect them or the public. One result of this criticism was a marked reduction in the numbers being sent particularly to Industrial Schools.' This was quoted from Parliamentary Papers 1896 [C.8204] XLV. It would take years, decades even, for this report to take effect on the Newcastle Industrial School, but take effect it did.

The schools were financially quite secure during these years; we can look at some of the figures. The workshops' profit in 1888 was £800, an admirable achievement. The schools' overall end-of-year balance was £1,084 3s 7d credit. In 1890 the credit balance was up to £1,670 14s 6d. Some of the capital was invested in 1891 in the North Eastern Railway's Preferential Stock, and in 1893 some more in Newcastle Corporation Stock. One teacher's salary was increased in 1893 from £110 p.a. to £125 p.a., and an old retired school nurse was granted a weekly pension.

Although this chapter has concentrated on Government legislation and its effects on the schools, I think it fitting that it end with more of the domestic details. These, after all, are what constituted the actual experiences of the teachers and children, workmasters and governors:

The governors' Annual General Meeting of 1889 took place on the school premises and was followed by a tour of the classrooms and workrooms to see the children at work. The children's tea was followed by some 'fireside stories from foreign lands' recounted by Mr Oliver, the Honorary Secretary of the Board.

In 1891 a gas-powered printing machine was bought.

The same year the children were taken to 'Mexican Joe's Entertainment' by an unnamed benefactor.

Effects of Old and New Legislation

All the beds were to be supplied with what sound very like interior sprung mattresses.

A few formal adoptions of children from the school took place in 1893, which attracted criticism.

One boy who had run away returned voluntarily; he had been working at a colliery. The school took him back and allowed him to work at the colliery 'on licence'.

A magic lantern had been bought.

All the children, in shifts, had had a fortnights' holiday at a the School's own seaside home in Whitley Bay.

One boy had been caught selling the firewood cut in the workshops.

Notes

1.   Report of the Commissioners on Reformatories and Industrial Schools, 1884.
2.   Cornish, W.R. and de N. Clark. *op. cit.* p.626.
3.   Cornish, W.R. and de N. Clark, G.: Law and society in England 1750-1950. (London, Sweet & Maxwell, 1989) p.625.

8

Trouble with Girls and the Beginnings of Decline

For the first time in a number of years 1896 saw a decline in profits from the workshops. Not a big decline – £789, compared with over £1,000 for the previous couple of years. There were fewer children in the schools of course since the new Board Schools were taking many children who would previously have been Ragged School pupils. In the case of the Newcastle Ragged and Industrial Schools these children had always been a majority. As we have seen, children committed by magistrates or the new School Boards were supposed to fill up the vacant places left (thus making the schools truly 'Industrial') but there were never enough of them. Ominously, Newcastle City Council had to withdraw its subscription owing to shortage of funds. In response, the schools requested a contribution from the School Board to the maintenance of 'committed' children. If the right hand could no longer give the money, perhaps the left hand could.

A nasty blow was dealt by the Printing Trades Union which announced its opposition to the commercial printing done by the boys' school and the print training done there. Its members would not employ any boy trained in the school. Ten years later it refused permission to Mr Linton, one of its members, to accept the post of printing teacher at the school.

With regard to repeated Home Office criticism of the kind of work done in the workshops, Mr Willoughby, the Superintendent, said in his 1896 report: 'the work done in the schools contributed very little direct training for situations [that the boys obtained on leaving]. [The schools] did not carry on ordnance work or engine building, and they had not a shipbuilding yard; but who could doubt the value of the simple work and labour which had enabled him to say to an employer that a lad knew nothing of the work it was proposed to put him to, but was a handy lad, steady and willing at his work, and had shown qualities which indicated that he would do well. The girls were trained for domestic service, and there was no difficulty in placing them – in fact the demand exceeded the supply.'

What industrial training to give continued to be a problem. There had been further pressure from the War Office to have boys trained for trade grades in the forces. The school committee decided to ignore this request, declaring it to be 'absolutely opposed to the most earnest views of those who founded the school'. This was stretching things: the founders had said nothing at all about the armed forces. Perhaps the committee feared that compliance would be the thin end of a wedge which would lead to the school putting the services' needs before the children's own or

The school's woodwork teacher with his equipage.

the wider society's. For a few years the boys were taught technical drawing but one Government Inspector criticised the teaching severely: the boys could draw well enough, he said, but they had no idea of the applications of the drawings. The classes ended. Many girls' Industrial Schools did laundry commercially and this work always brought in a profit; more than once the Newcastle Schools considered it. The nearby Whitley Cottage Homes for Girls were already doing laundry even though they were a much newer enterprise than the Industrial Schools. In the event no commercial laundry was started at the Newcastle School because of the falling numbers of girls, a matter we will examine later.

The daily timetable of schooling and training was occasionally applied less than rigorously. In what sounds like a jolly break from routine one day in 1897 the boys' teaching was foregone for a whole day whilst teachers and boys alike packed a large cargo of Swedish timber. Presumably some importer paid the school for this work.

In spite of difficulties over Board School truants and official criticism of the industrial training, the schools continued to be successful. For one thing, in 1897 their scholastic attainments were finally on a level with the Board Schools'. And in the summer a brilliant Jubilee garden party was held in Jesmond Dene to celebrate fifty years of the school's life and sixty years of Queen Victoria's reign. The sad death of Lord Armstrong brought a blessing to the school in the form of a £500 bequest. In 1900 a telephone was installed: each outgoing call would cost 1d. Unfortunately in 1902 it was vandalised. 1902 was a rather miserable year for other reasons. The profit from firewood was lower than usual as there were a lot of competing producers, and the growing popularity of gas fires meant less demand for firewood. That summer was cold and wet and the annual outing was cancelled. But mostly the news was good.

A quayside timber importer.

On January 31, 1901 the *Newcastle Daily Leader* ran an article on the schools, including the following:

> *The Newcastle Ragged and Industrial School – which has long since ceased to justify the first portion of its description, for it has become wholly industrial – flourishes wonderfully. The investments are more than £20,000 and on the income of £4,200 received in 1900 there is a balance of £1,015. The technical side of the establishment produced a profit in 1900 of £1,065, a record in the fifty-three years' career of the schools. Those of the inmates who have gone out into the workaday world have, with very few exceptions, acquitted themselves with infinite credit. One girl has been singularly fortunate. Her late mistress, whom she served twenty years, esteemed her so highly as to make her joint legatee with her own sister of her (the mistress') estate.*

A gymnasium for the boys was built in the early years of the new century, partly with the help of an American philanthropist, Mr Hilton Philipson, who pledged an annual contribution of £25. The boys took to the new sport with keenness, and by 1905 gymnastic displays were frequent. By 1906 a regional competition had been established with a silver cup, the 'Ravensworth Challenge Cup' as prize.

News from old pupils continued to come in. One 'old boy' now owned five shops and employed fifty men; another, astonishingly, had become a professor at Aberdeen University.

Middle-class children in Jesmond Dene.

One wonders whether 'professor' had the same meaning then as now; if so it was truly an outstanding achievement. Another boy who had left thirty years ago was now, and had been for fifteen years, editor of the *West Cumbrian Times*.

An interesting detail from these years is that the National School Board, having refused to allow the Newcastle School to operate as a Day Industrial School as well as a boarding school, had opened its own, but after a very few years had had to close it as uneconomic. One can guess it regretted its earlier decision.

Dental inspections and treatment, and the same for eyes, were added in these years to the medical care the schools already provided. Since the services of dentists cost the schools £10 yearly we may assume no financial troubles. But a decline had already begun, which could not be ignored.

For some time the number of girls committed to Industrial Schools had been falling. In 1902 the Newcastle Schools had only thirty-two girls, and by the time of the Annual Report for 1903 only twenty-six – compared with 149 boys. It is easy to see why the building of a separate girls' school 'to specification' might not be seen as a priority: what if the number of girls were to diminish to zero? That year's Annual Report said: 'The diminution in numbers of girls is general to Industrial Schools in the city and neighbourhood, and it is not easy to determine the cause'. (Six years later a damning report on the conditions of the girls' lives in the school would give a good explanation). Why was the committee so apparently blind to the hardship of the girls' lives?

It was probably because they could not bear to admit any fault in their flourishing project. The schools were a success; faith and risks had been justified. Anyone looking for faults must be mean-spirited and lacking vision! But the committee must have known that Industrial Schools and Reformatories were beginning to lose their patina of excellence in both the public's eyes and the Government's. And most of the 'horror stories' concerned girls' establishments.

Growing numbers of magistrates preferred to put a first-time offending girl on probation or at least to send her to a Village Home. Village Homes were a new initiative thought better suited to girls than large Industrial Schools. They consisted of houses arranged to imitate a village, each house with its own housemother and housefather; the girls' lives were modelled as far as possible on ordinary family life. Some of the homes had Industrial School status, some did not, in which case their girls attended local schools. Their very existence suggests that the old model of Industrial Schools for girls would not last much longer. Northumberland Village Homes, set up and run by the Girls' Friendly Society, were becoming a preferred choice for first-offending girls in the Newcastle area. It is interesting that the schools' Minutes never specifically mentioned the Village Homes as a reason for their own falling rolls of girls, nor do they mention probation, perhaps because they did not want to see the way the wind was blowing.

In 1904 magistrates were invited to inspect the Newcastle Schools, perhaps in the hope of persuading them to commit more girls. There were contributory reasons for the loss of girls. For instance, police no longer took children before a magistrate simply for being 'vagrant', but only if they were caught committing a crime. Since females always and everywhere commit fewer crimes than males, fewer of them would be committed to the Newcastle School.

No Minutes from these years show the governors ever wondering whether the hard life of girls at the schools was a reason magistrates were loath to send them there. After all, the girls were washing clothes and bedding by hand, albeit with the help of a 'washing machine' from 6 a.m. throughout the whole day, washing for both boys' and girls' schools, staff and pupils, with only short breaks for meals and lessons. It is shocking that the Ladies' Committee voted against buying an additional washing machine to lighten the girls' load, even when the schools were prosperous! In the light of this onerous life it is extraordinary that in 1896 the girls outperformed the boys in the annual examinations: 98 per cent passing compared with 97 per cent, and in 1899 two girls won scholarships to the Domestic Science College in Eldon Square. Two others in the same year won prizes in an essay competition arranged by the SPCA (forerunner of the RSPCA), which shows that they could write well despite having so little time for it.

Another reason already mentioned for the decrease in girls' numbers was a growing dislike for mixed-sex institutions. This sentiment had been influencing society for some decades and had shown itself in novels of the period. For instance, in Zola's *Germinal* the employment of women in mines was thought shocking as much for the indecency as the hardship (women had to work half-undressed because of the heat, and this presented an unfair temptation to the men). One way and another it seemed that the Newcastle Schools would lose their girl pupils and thus their unpaid laundresses.

The growing concern of the state over the welfare of children expressed itself in a Governmental 'Children's Charter' which, amongst other things, established special Juvenile Courts in 1908. Finally, in 1909, came a Home Office Inspector's Report which forced the Newcastle School's Board of Governors to face facts. It took the form of a letter to the chairman which I quote here in full.

Whitley Bay Village Homes.

Home Office, S.W.
2nd April, 1909

Dear Mr Oliver,

My lady colleague, Mrs Harrison, recently paid a visit to the Girls' Department of the Industrial School and spent a long day there going carefully through the whole arrangements. The result of her visit was to convince her that the girls have too much to do and that, to make matters worse, a great deal of their hard work is crowded into the time before and the time after school, e.g., a girl goes into the laundry soon after six in the morning, leaves off for prayers and breakfast and then returns until noon when she takes a quarter of an hour for dinner, and again returns to the laundry until six o'clock when on Monday evening she leaves off to take cookery until eight o'clock or on Friday to scrub dining-room tables and then to the laundry again to fold clothes. More washing is done on Saturday forenoon and evening. This appears to be a very hard life for children who, with two exceptions, are under fifteen years of age. Seeing that there are only about twent-seven girls in all it seems unreasonable for them to undertake more than the washing of their own clothes and possibly those of their own staff. Seeing that they are comparatively young children they should not be expected to work in the laundry after tea-time, nor even after dinner-time on Saturdays. I would suggest that machinery might be introduced into the laundry either on one side or other of the school for the rough washing, and also that the three hours system of schooling for half the girls at one time should be adopted as is generally the case throughout Industrial Schools. It would also be as well if drill lessons were continued through the summer as well as the winter. Possibly a woman might be engaged to help in the washing, especially for the boys. Under the present arrangements the life of the girls seems to be one of drudgery, and

Newcastle Ragged and Industrial School

I am sure I have only to draw the attention of the Committee to the matter for it to receive their fullest and sympathetic consideration. Of course another alternative which I put forward with all diffidence is to find a separate establishment for the girls and carry on Jubilee Road as a Boys' School only.

With kind regards, and hoping that you will kindly lay this letter before the Committee,

Yours very truly
[signed] T.W. Robertson.

This letter says it all, and one might be amazed that Mr Robertson could adopt so mild a tone. I rather suspect Mrs Harrison was angrier when she made her original report to him. Of course things would not always have been so bad for the girls; before their numbers fell there would have been more hands to do the work. On the other hand there would have been more washing to do. How the committee managed to ignore such patent hardship is hard to understand: even the human reluctance to see faults in one's treasured project usually melts before incontrovertible evidence. The Minutes of the Ladies' Committee for 1909 perfectly illustrated this 'look-the-other-way' attitude. They mentioned in passing the Lady Inspector's visit and her criticism of the girls' workload, but with no hint of shame or apology. The matter was casually included in a paragraph glowing with self-congratulation for 'another successful year'. A later paragraph mentioned, again by the way, that three women had been taken on to do the boys' washing. And a long-standing proposal to buy an additional washing machine had at last been agreed to. In other words the criticisms had found their mark and the necessary improvements been made but with no breath of *mea culpa* from anybody. It was as though the Inspector's visit and Mr Robertson's letter were no more than annoying embarassments which unfortunately could not be ignored.

The Home Office letter brought to a head the whole question of a girls' school, whether on shared or separate premises. Since the number of girls committed by magistrates continued to dwindle, should the whole enterprise of a girls' school be given up? The Newcastle Schools were now the only mixed-sex Industrial Schools in the country. Eventually there was a meeting at the Home Office at which Mr Robertson (the same who had written the letter) ordered that the school was to admit no more girls. The girls already there were to be licensed out to work (if old enough) or transferred to other schools. But – and this was stressed – all such placements, whether to employers or other schools, must be examined and passed as suitable first, if necessary by the Home Office itself. There was to be no 'dumping' of girls just to get them off the school's hands. In the event some of the girls went to the Whitley Village Homes and some to the Sunderland Girls' Industrial School. From this date onwards the Newcastle School was a boys' school only.

The Annual Report of 1910 was mealy-mouthed about the closing of the girls' school. The damning letter from the Home Office was not mentioned; instead there were quantities of the phrases that come so easily to the English: 'due regret' 'splendid results' 'many years' hard work' etc. It is true that many of the girls had turned out well, and that in some years they had had a reasonable amount of teaching and perhaps a bit of leisure. It is also true though that their lives even in good years had been harder than the boys', and that the Committees, especially the Ladies' Committee, had not been perturbed by this. This cannot be entirely explained by the absence of women's rights, because the Ladies' Committee itself suffered the same disadvantage. I suggest the reason was a combination of the still depressed position of women with a persisting *ancien regime* attitude toward the poor.

With the girls no longer on hand to do the washing free, the school planned an entire new laundry equipped with machines! How strange, or rather how typical that this had not occurred to anyone earlier.

9

Reorganisation and the Move to Axwell Park

By 1911 the number of boys being admitted was falling. There were now competing alternatives to prison for young offenders, most notably probation. Introduced in 1887, its scope had been widened in 1907, and by 1911 was the preferred method of dealing with juvenile first offenders provided certain safeguards were met. It is as well to point out here that committal to an Industrial School had always been simply one option open to magistrates, who were not legally bound to order it. Between 10 December 1910 and the writing of the 1911 Annual Report only six boys were committed to the Newcastle Industrial School, all of them truancy cases. Reformatories suffered the same drop in admissions for the same reasons.

In 1911 the Newcastle School published an account of the subsequent histories of all pupils who had left between about 1870 and 1910. In the case of boys the total was 5,803. Of these 1,071 of these had become farm workers, 481 miners, 886 had gone into the Army, including many former band players, 163 into the Royal Navy [a small number because the Navy was highly selective of its recruits], 246 into the Merchant Navy, 217 into factories, 337 were general labourers and 123 casual labourers. The rest (about 1,000) were spread over every variety of trade. No notable high achievement was mentioned, such as had marked the lives of school leavers in the early years. There were 276 boys whose whereabouts and occupations were 'unknown', 199 had been convicted and either were or had been in prison or transported.

The total of girls who had left in these years was 1,564. Of these 639 had become general servants, 154 were employed in casual labour, usually cleaning, 133 were housemaids, 78 were working in factories or mills, 118 were laundry-maids, in both private and public institutions, 29 were married, 62 were nursemaids. The remainder (about 300) were employed in a variety of 'female' jobs [perhaps shop assistants or machinists] although 73 were 'unknown' and 9 had been convicted. Once again, no 'star' 'old girls'.

It seems clear that by this date the schools were past their best. The reasons for their decline will be examined later. The Minutes for 1912 were sparse though they did record that the fund originally set up to establish a convalescent home for 'old girls' could be drawn on now by the school for any purpose, since there were no longer any girl pupils.

In 1913 the Home Office produced a new Report on Reformatories and Industrial Schools which deserves to be studied in detail, as it set in train measures which, over the following

Axwell Park, to which the boys' school moved.

two decades, changed the Industrial Schools so radically that they were no longer the same institutions.

It pointed out first and foremost that in future Industrial Schools would be in short supply because it was highly unlikely any new ones would be built. The 1908 Children's Act had imposed on local authorities the duty of financially maintaining children committed to Industrial Schools (rather than, as previously, the option), but no single authority had enough such children in its remit now to justify building a school for them. This was because changes in the law relating to juvenile offenders had produced alternative penalties. Where committals were made therefore, existing Industrial Schools would have to be used. But these were losing their benefactors, who saw no point in supporting such schools when elementary education for all, technical education for those who could benefit, and Government schemes for young offenders were already in place, paid for through taxes. The Home Office had no power to build Industrial Schools itself, only to certify and regulate them and contribute to their maintenance. It did however have the power to close down such schools as failed to meet the required standard: a power it had used in the past and could use again. But this course of action now had a huge drawback: if poor schools were forced to close there would soon be nowhere to go for the kind of children they accepted. The report advised Home Office Inspectors to be chary of heavy criticism because Industrial Schools only existed at all 'with the goodwill of, and co-operation from, benefactors'. The power of closure should only be used in extremity.

One can see immediately that this was a licence for bad schools to continue unreformed. And there certainly were bad schools. The report noted this fact euphemistically as 'great variations between schools'. Especially in some rural areas there was not much public interest in the schools and therefore no watch kept upon them. Unless a keen and active Management Committee was present 'there is always a danger of the Superintendents and officers becoming slack and spiritless, or even allowing abuses and malpractices to creep into the school'.

The report stressed that the character of a school's Superintendent was paramount. Some Industrial School Superintendents were excellent, others though too old or simply incompetent despite good intentions. The teachers were overworked. They should live out where possible so as not to be constantly on call. Married male teachers should be preferred over unmarried. (This might be a veiled hint at the dangers of homosexuality or perhaps a swipe at the Christian Brothers who staffed some of the Roman Catholic Industrial Schools and had a reputation for harshness.)

The education in the schools was found to be 'like the best elementary schools of fifteen or twenty years ago.' (By this date state elementary schools had existed for forty-three years.) Some Inspectors gave their subversive opinion that such teaching was better than the new 'creative' kind which was just being introduced into the state schools!

A major recommendation was that half-time teaching should be for over-twelves only. No younger child should work in the workshops but instead should have the day devoted to education. Education however could include handicrafts as taught in the board's elementary schools. Even for the over-twelves, teaching time was not to be sacrificed to rough unproductive work with no educational content. Nor must schoolwork be pushed to the ends of the days: early morning, late afternoon. And neither learning nor work should start before breakfast. The senior pupils' curriculum should resemble the Education Board's Evening Continuation Schools. Here in this recommendation we see fade like a shadow one of the schools' founding aims: to teach children habits of work

A stern note was sounded in the report's pronouncements on Physical Education and Games. PE should not aim to produce a small group of elite gymnasts to win prizes. (This sounds directly aimed at the Newcastle School and its Ravensworth Challenge Cup). Smaller, weaker boys should not be made to do hard exercises. Swedish Drill was strongly recommended for both sexes. PE should include dancing, relay races, and beanbag games. Older boys could exercise on apparatus so long as the exercise was not aimed at what we nowadays would call bodybuilding. (One wonders what the Newcastle School's boys made of being offered beanbag games and dancing instead of the gymnastics challenge cup!).

It was noted that the constant stream of newcomers into Industrial Schools, most of them Board School truants and many almost fourteen (the school-leaving age) and therefore staying only a short time, had a negative influence on community spirit. Moreover some of these short-stay boys were 'hardened', i.e. already involved in petty crime, and their example undid the moral good work effected on the long-stay boys. Nor could these 'bad' pupils be refused admission because the Industrial Schools relied on the grant money that came with them!

The diet was criticised as was the crowding in dining rooms and the chipped plates and cups. The practice of bathing children together in batches was condemned along with the wearing of hobnailed boots and 'convict' caps. (As far as we can tell the Newcastle School's pupils had never worn such boots or caps but perhaps they had been bathed in batches).

This report's chief criticism however was aimed at the Reformatories. These had originally been set up around the same time as Industrial Schools and had been intended to take children over twelve (later fourteen) who had served a prison sentence at some time. This meant that the shelter and education they provided had never been available to neglected street youngsters of that age who were on the edge of crime but who had not been to prison. Such boys and girls were simply older versions of the children sent to Industrial Schools but because of their age they could not go there.

The report's chief recommendation was that the distinction between Reformatories and

Industrial Schools should be done away with. There should be simply Junior and Senior Home Office Schools. The Junior Schools, i.e. what had been the Industrial Schools, would admit children under fourteen who had been convicted even of many offences provided these were not serious. This was a major departure from the founders' intention, which had been to save 'untainted' children who had committed one offence only and never been in prison. Over-fourteens would go to the Senior Schools (what had been the Reformatories) even if they had committed only one offence. Thus a new distinction was drawn by age only, rather than the old one between 'innocent' and 'hardened'. It would be decades before these recommendations were fully acted upon but they spelled out the future direction of the schools from that year forward.

One further recommendation was that the admission of little children, far too young for industrial training and often too young for schooling, should be stopped. We know from Gertrude Tuckwell that one of the London Industrial Schools had admitted a three-year-old boy 'found wandering'. He became 'a great pet' of the older girls. Industrial Schools were advised in this report not to admit any further children under eight years, and magistrates were being instructed not to commit such children.[1] Other recommendations were for additional annual inspections and for these to always include a woman Inspector who would be better at noticing physical details.

It is clear from this report that the days of the Industrial Schools in their old form were numbered. Paradoxically though, the same report showed that in the short term, i.e. years immediately following 1913, Industrial Schools were still needed.

Since the Government itself was not prepared to build and staff Industrial Schools it must continue for the time being to make use of existing ones even if they consistently failed to meet Government standards. It was an insoluble problem.

The Newcastle School, now only a boys' school, was still in place and functioning in 1914, and complying with the new Government requirements. For instance, it issued in that year new details of the boys' diet, of which a summary follows:

Breakfast: Sunday, Monday, Wednesday, Thursday, Friday: Cocoa, bread and dripping. There was a choice of coffee on Thursday. Tuesday and Saturday: Porridge with ½ pint milk and ½ oz Sugar. Bread.

Dinner Sunday: potato soup made with bones, bread. Monday: boiled beef or mutton, barley, potatoes, bread. Tuesday: Irish stew, vegetables, potatoes, bread. Wednesday: pea soup, barley, vegetables, bread. Thursday: roast beef, vegetables, potatoes, bread. Friday: suet pudding with treacle or stewed fruit. Saturday: minced beef, potatoes, vegetables, bread.

Tea Sunday: bread and margarine, occasionally cake, tea. Monday: bread and margarine, cocoa or coffee. Tuesday: bread and dripping, cocoa. Wednesday: bread and jam, cocoa. Thursday: bread and dripping, cocoa. Friday: bread and jam, tea. Saturday: bread and dripping, cocoa.

In addition bread and cocoa was served every morning except Sunday at 6.15 a.m. [i.e. well before breakfast]. This would have been to comply with the new requirement that children should not start work or lessons without food first. Bread and biscuits were served each evening as a 'supper' at 8.15 p.m. every day except Sunday.

Quantities per pupil per meal were given:

Bread 8 oz (breakfast and tea), 4 oz (dinner)
Cocoa ¾ pint, including ¼ milk
Tea ¾ pint, including ¼ pint milk
Dripping ¾ oz.
Margarine ¾ oz.
Jam 1 oz
Meat 4 oz raw weight
Potatoes 8 oz
Vegetables 4 oz
Barley 1 oz
Pudding 8 oz.

This diet was an improvement on the earlier one, most notably by the inclusion of vegetables, and certainly no Inspector could criticise it for lack of quantity. I doubt I myself could eat eight ounces of suet pudding with treacle, even as a main course.

No further Annual Reports of the school are available, but we know that in 1920 it bought the house and grounds of Axwell Park, across the river at Blaydon-on-Tyne, and in June 1922 moved there. In 1919 the Home Office had reformed the funding of Industrial Schools so that they received most of their finance from the Home Office itself and local authorities. I suspect this was done to stop the schools relying on the children's labour to bring money in. If I am right it meant that one more of the founders' aims had been abandoned. We have evidence however that the new funding arrangements still did not meet needs, and appeals for benefactions continued into the 1930s.

T.A. Robinson, who became one of the headmasters during the school's later history at Axwell Park, wrote, post 1948, a pamphlet entitled *Brief History of Axwell Park School* 1848 – 1948, from which I now quote:

> Soon after the First World War committals to the Industrial and Reformatory Schools decreased rapidly and many of them were only half-filled. Many closed. This was when the Newcastle Industrial School decided to move to Axwell Park. Alterations cost £50,000, met by sale of old premises, investments etc. There was no begging from the Home Office. The four following Industrial Schools in the north-east closed, and the remaining boys in [them] sent to Axwell Park: Durham, Sunderland, Middlesbrough, Gateshead.

An unsigned letter exists addressed to a Mr Forsbee, dated 3 June 1931, which seems to be answering a request for information:

> This school was opened as a Ragged School for 50 boys in Sandgate, Newcastle-upon-Tyne, on the 11th August 1847 and in the following year was moved to more commodious premises in Gibson Street.
>
> A new school was erected in New Road, Newcastle, and opened on the 24th January 1855 and continued there until 30th June 1922, when it moved to Axwell Park, Blaydon-on-Tyne.
>
> The school was certified by Sir C.B. Adderley, Vice-President of HM Privy Council on Education on the 3rd June 1859 as an Industrial School under the first English Industrial Schools Act (1857) and became known as the Newcastle-upon-Tyne Ragged and Industrial Schools. On the removal of the school in 1922 the management decided to name it The Axwell Park School.

Sandgate at the time the school moved out of Newcastle.

It is certified for 150 boys and 2,272 have passed through the school. It may be termed a resident elementary school. The teachers are trained and certified and schoolroom work is organised under the three departments, Senior (students VI and VII), Middle (Students IV and V), and Junior (Preparatory to Student III). The School is regularly inspected by the board of Education Inspectors as well as by those of the Home Office.

All boys in the Senior and Middle Divisions receive instruction in woodwork, and special boys receive lessons in bookbinding. Further training is given in the Joiner's Shop, the House Decorating and Painting Class, and in the Market Garden.

The general working of the school is on the house system, and there are four houses with house masters and prefects. There is ample scope for sports and games as the School stands in 60 acres of land, a part of which would be utilized and developed for farming and poultry farming except for lack of funds.

It is clear that great reorganisation must have gone on in the years for which we have no Annual Reports.

Notes

1. Tuckwell, Gertrude, *op. cit.* Quoted in Sanders, Wiley B. *op. cit.* p.305.

10

The Axwell Park Years

Axwell Park had a picturesque setting high on the north bank of the river Derwent; it had originally belonged to a retired colonel. From the letter and pamphlet quoted we see the school was quite different from the old Jubilee Road one, more like a minor Public School in fact. And within a few years it came under the control as well as the financing of the Newcastle Board of Education plus the Home Office, although some subscriptions continued. It carried on with mixed fortunes for more than a decade, but since it was a different creature from the old Industrial School I will only deal summarily with these later years.

The letter to Mr Forsbee, quoted earlier, ended with a request for funds to provide a swimming bath, a gymnasium and a sports pavilion, so clearly benefactions were still being sought. By 1931 the school was struggling financially, selling off buildings and plots of land. The market gardening had proved unprofitable, with hardly any boys finding work as gardeners when they left.

We have Axwell Park's diaries for 1928 – 33, which take the form of the headmaster's log books. It is from these documents that the whole of what follows is taken, except where another source is indicated. We learn that in 1928 the boys did their own darning and mending and cleaned their own living quarters. When one reflects, it is strange that at the mixed school in Jubilee Road the girls were expected to wash and clean for the boys; after all, soldiers and sailors do these things for themselves. At Axwell Park the boys had several woodwork classes each week, and on Wednesdays this was devoted to repairs around the school. The aim of being self-supporting in as many ways as possible was obviously still alive even though allotted much less time than in the old school.

The boys were taken to the cinema every week, and a doctor and dentist was available on request as well as to perform annual inspections. Sunday afternoons were free; this meant the boys 'boarding' in their own homes could go home if they wished: the others went for walks or played games. The band was flourishing with band practice many evenings. On the first day of each new term those boys who had been home for the holidays were given a bath and change of clothes. The concession of a child 'boarding' with his parents or other suitable adults, if approved, rather than at school – a concession which had been present from the second Industrial Schools Act (1861) – was still in place. It obviously saved the Home Office and Board of Education money to have children boarded at home so long as this did not compromise their welfare.

There were worries about the gardening, which was making no profit. This shows that the aim of training children to work for money had not been abandoned at Axwell Park even if it had elsewhere. The entry for 2 March reads 'No school today. Had all boys in the ploughed fields tidying up' (this was a potato field). One wonders what the Newcastle Board of Education said about that! Or indeed about 3 May when, said the headmaster, the whole school worked in the gardens until 8.15 p.m. In fact throughout May the whole school except the very youngest boys sometimes spent all day gardening and regularly every evening, even – and this is stressed as extraordinary – even the bandboys! By 6 June the potato field at least was 'finished'.

There was Church Parade every Sunday and on other occasions such as Empire Day. The national flag was carried and solemnly saluted as part of these parades. On the last Wednesday in June a traditional Newcastle holiday, Race Wednesday, was held; it was part of the old miners' Race Week. The Axwell Park boys were excused afternoon school and many took an extended leave until 9 p.m.

Each July the school went camping for a number of weeks. The year 1928 had a wet summer and the campers returned to school on 3 August. Until September they were still theoretically on summer holiday; in fact they worked at yet more gardening, not just in the fields but in a 'Horticultural Pleasure Garden'. Perhaps there was an idea of admitting the public for a fee. The gardening staff must have been unsatisfactory as it was decided to replace them.

The usual staff apart from the headmaster were a principal teacher, assistant teachers, a manual instructor, gardeners, a matron, and domestic staff including 'sewing maids'. So perhaps the boys did not do all their own mending after all.

A laconic entry for 16 September reads: '16 boys absconded during the afternoon'! But by the 23rd the last of them had returned to school. Absconding was common, boys usually escaping

Flower gardens at Axwell Park.

in twos and threes for a few days. As often as not they gave themselves up. The offence was not thought serious although – and this comes as a surprise – it was punished by caning. There had been no mention of caning in the Jubilee Road school. Boys sometimes tried to stow away on ships; one repeat stowaway had got as far as Dartmouth! Repeat offenders were put on a bread-and-water diet for a few days as punishment.

The school was careful about its pastoral role. For instance, one boy who had left normally was subsequently 'licensed' and recalled to the school as 'work has not yet been found for him and as he is of very poor intellect it is to his advantage to remain here longer.'

The whole school went to Newcastle on 10 October to see the king and queen open 'the new bridge'. On Christmas Eve 'Santa Claus visited dormitories at midnight' and on Christmas Day there was a traditional Christmas dinner. Many visitors came, including 'old boys'. There were games in the afternoon.

In January 1929 a radio was bought and all the school listened to the enthronement of the Archbishop of Canterbury. That month saw heavy snowfalls so the boys went sledging. A cold frosty February resulted in burst pipes, putting the boiler out of action. It was not properly repaired until April and even then the heating system did not function well. One wonders how they kept warm: perhaps with coal fires or paraffin heaters.

There were regular sporting fixtures against other schools; the headmaster claimed that Axwell won most of the football matches, but lost most of the cricket, especially, surprisingly, when playing against the *Wellesley* Training Ship.

A fair number of boys joined the Army on leaving, and some, if they wished it, were taken direct from school to the Recruiting Officer. This did not necessarily mean a settled future: the headmaster was often called to court to testify about 'old boys' who had deserted the Army – or who had committed criminal offences.

The school had an 'Auxiliary Home'. No details are given but, reading between the lines, we can guess that it was either a 'halfway house' for boys of leaving age who were not yet able to support themselves, or perhaps a lodge for 'old boys' fallen on hard times.

The radio was proving its worth; amongst other things the boys listened in to the Naval Armaments Conference and the Cenotaph service in November 1930. In the same year boys watched planes passing overhead making for Cramlington in the King's Cup race.

In April the school admitted twenty-four boys transferred from the Abbott Memorial School, another sign that Industrial School provision was being rationalized, in other words reduced. In May one pupil was transferred to Rampton high security hospital by order of the Secretary of State: no details of his offence are given but it must have been serious and repeated. There were occasional accidents at the school as anywhere else; in one a boy lost an eye by walking into a metal fixture in the lavatories at night. There were acts of petty vandalism and occasionally a more serious crime demanding visits from detectives. The school had become a typical young offenders' institution.

There were domestic troubles in plenty, particularly over staff dismissals and staff wages. The sewing-room maids and the cook seemed to figure largely in these. To add to the troubles in August 1933 fire broke out on the school's farm and it took 15,600 gallons of water to put it out.

November 23 1933 saw a conference of managers and heads of Industrial Schools together with Home Office officials in London. No report of the discussions was given, but we can safely surmise they concerned the change of name from Industrial Schools (and Reformatories) to Approved Schools. This was simply the *coup de grace*; it will be plain from the Axwell Park diaries that the institutions were by this date far more concerned with the training of juvenile

Axwell Park in the early twentieth century.

offenders than with the 'saving' of 'perishing' children from a life of crime. The training of juvenile offenders was in its turn attracting disapproval from progressive quarters. According to Cornish and de N. Clark, a Departmental Committee on Young Offenders of 1925-1927 was chiefly preoccupied with deciding the merits of rival progressive theories and its important recommendations formed the basis of legislation in 1932. A footnote informs that the resulting Act was consolidated in 1933 into the Children and Young Persons Act. This was the Act which ended Industrial Schools once and for all. By this date Axwell Park could no longer be regarded as a private benevolent enterprise or even a Newcastle civic one; it was already in essence just what the Home Office wanted.

11
Conclusions

The Industrial Schools had three aims which, although perhaps not kept distinct in the minds of their founders, we can separate and examine. From this examination we may find reasons for what happened to the schools.

The first aim was expressed loftily by their founders as the saving of perishing and destitute children from a life of crime. More cynically it could be seen as providing humane punishment for young first-time lawbreakers. The second aim was to give these children elementary education. The third was to teach them how to work and earn their living. I contend that this third ambition was flawed in ways I will make clear.

First let us look at Industrial Schools as a humane punishment for young first-time lawbreakers. As we saw, from about 1857, when the first Industrial Schools Act was passed, to 1887 when the Probation of First Offenders Act was passed, the schools were a popular choice for magistrates faced with young first offenders.

Industrial School certification was also a popular choice for the many charitable enterprises set up to 'save' street children. We have seen that the Newcastle School began as a Ragged School. In Liverpool, St George's Industrial School began as a boys' Refuge. And if certification was desired because of the *per capita* Government grant that went with it, what was the harm in that? The Government itself gained because it would have had to spend money on lodging the children in prison had there been no Industrial Schools. And, from the Government's point of view, these schools were an experiment that might work whereas the prisons, with a few notable exceptions, had been shown not to work.

Towards the end of the century however a revolt began against the faith in institutions which had marked so much of early Victorian reform. I suspect this was not unconnected with the growing distaste on the part of the intelligentsia for factory production with its huge sheds of human automata (as they would describe it) and the longing for a mythical simpler life which found its apotheosis in the Arts and Crafts movement. Whether or not I am right, large boarding-school-type establishments such as Industrial Schools and Reformatories began to fall into disfavour. Their cause was not helped by a series of scandals of one sort or another. So far as we know the Newcastle School's blithe disregard of its girls pupils' overwork and misery in these later years did not make a story in the newspapers, but other more egregious examples did. Certainly in Scotland the 'steamies', commercial laundries operated by Reformatory girls, were notorious.

Newcastle Ragged and Industrial School

Almost from the beginning some Industrial Schools were organised as 'Village Homes', that is, as groups of small households each supposed to resemble a family home. In the late nineteenth century, where Industrial School sentences were given, these 'Village Homes' were preferred over other establishments.

What about the educational ambitions of the Industrial Schools? The Reports of Inspectors from the Council of Education in the early years and the Home Office later have to be believed because we have nothing with which to challenge them. According to these reports many Industrial Schools, including the Newcastle ones, taught very well considering the original state of the children they took. I think we can safely bet that no girl or boy, even if of low intelligence, left the Newcastle Ragged and Industrial Schools functionally illiterate.

The 1870 Elementary Education Act put an end, over time, to the *raison d'etre* of the Ragged Schools. As we have seen, many Industrial Schools started as Ragged Schools and continued to take non-sentenced children even after certification as Industrial: Newcastle was one. Ragged Schools were well supported by public philanthropy and civic treasuries. But once the 1870 Act established elementary schools countrywide, people saw no need to continue these donations. After all, the Government's new Board Schools were financed out of general taxation. So numbers of Ragged School pupils began a terminal decline in those schools, like Newcastle, which were a combination of Ragged and Industrial. However, those civic councils which decided to make elementary education compulsory, and Newcastle was one, soon had a massive truancy problem, which they solved partly by sending the truants to Industrial Schools on a magistrate's order. Thus, the 1870 Act took away from the combined Ragged-and-Industrial Schools on one hand and gave something with the other. But what was given was a stream of short-stay children who often disrupted the day-to-day atmosphere. As a result the overall ethos of the schools changed.

We now come to the third of the Industrial Schools' objectives, namely, to teach children to work and eventually support themselves. This is the one I find most problematic, although I am not opposed in principle to children working for money. The trouble with the Industrial Schools was that they wanted to teach general work skills rather than specific trades and at the same time to make money. As we know, they all did end up teaching particular trades, notably tailoring and bootmaking, and, in the case of the Newcastle School, printing. But for reasons we have seen none of these crafts became reliable moneymakers for any of the schools. Were they then a good apprenticeship for earning one's living? Articles made but not sold might be good practice in one skill or another but certainly not good practice in earning money. Therefore it could be said that only profitable work could count as work in this particular context. But the work that was profitable was the least skilled and most arduous: woodchopping in the case of boys, laundry in the case of girls. So the children could either make money from unpleasant work or learn to sew a fine seam in a suit nobody would buy.

Despite contradictions in the theory, as we have seen great numbers of the Newcastle School boys and girls went on to be successful in their working lives, especially in the early years. These would be years when many of the children were Ragged School pupils, not young first offenders; it is possible therefore that they would have made a go of life no matter which school they had attended. Nevertheless, as the Newcastle Schools were the ones they did attend they can justly claim some credit.

It is interesting that the worst episode in the Newcastle Schools' history was traceable not to faults in the underlying theories nor in the application of those theories but to deep-seated beliefs so widespread at the time as to be unquestioned: namely the general attitude to women, and the feeling that the poor, although they should be helped, should not be regarded in the

Many boys went into the Merchant Navy.

same light as one's own family and friends. Thus, poor girls should be grateful that anything at all was done for them. Fifteen minutes to eat dinner? Certainly one could not eat one's own dinner in that time nor ask one's own daughter to do so, but these girls were poor and as such should be glad to have a dinner at all. One sometimes hears faint echoes of these sentiments even today.

In conclusion I must say that I experienced something whilst researching this book that was quite unexpected and, upon reflection, both profound and banal. It was a sense of living through, at fast-forward speed, the lives of people long dead. The visionary original benefactors grew old, sickened (their apologies for absence recorded in the Minutes) and died. Sometimes their sons took on the responsibility of the school, the same names occurring over time on the committee. They in their turn aged and died; I watched the vision of the school grow paler with the years. The thousands of children who passed through the schools and went out into the world to become my and your ancestors seemed to be around me, and I wept for young James Murray, fired with commitment to his charges, cut down in his prime by the 'Irish plague'. So many lives, whether long or short, as full of passion and significance as my own. Indeed my final gratitude goes to them for allowing me to move among them.

Newcastle waterfront in the early twentieth century.

Bibliography and References

Acts of Parliament and Government reports:

Juvenile Offenders Act 1847
House of Commons Select Committee Report on criminal and destitute children, 21 May 1852
Industrial Schools Act 1857
Industrial Schools Act 1861
Elementary Education Act 1870
Compulsory Elementary Education Act 1892
Report of the Departmental Committee on Reformatories and Industrial Schools 1913

Original material:

Axwell Park Approved School Headmasters' Log Books 1928-33. [Handwritten in hardbacked exercise book]

Elsdon, B.W.: *Speech urging a Day Industrial School at a meeting of Gateshead School Board* Feb. 14 1877. [Anonymously printed]

Newcastle Borough (later City) Council Annual Minutes 1847-1900

Newcastle Ragged and Industrial Schools Annual Reports 1848-1914 [incomplete]

Newcastle Ragged and Industrial Schools Minutes of monthly meeting of the Committee 1847-1912 [incomplete]

Newcastle Ragged and Industrial Schools Monthly minutes of Ladies' Committee 1855-1909 [incomplete]

Newcastle Ragged and Industrial Schools Log book of punishments [handwritten in hardbacked exercise books]

Watson, R.J.: *Industrial Schools* (pamphlet printed at Newcastle Ragged and Industrial Schools 1867).

Other sources:

Altick, R.D.: *The English common reader: a social history,* 1800-1900 (University of Chicago Press 1957)

[Anon.]: A brief history of Axwell Park School in [a record of] Axwell Park School Centenary Annual Meeting, 16 June 1948

Approved Schools Gazette December 1966

Bentham, Jeremy: *Works,* vol. 1 ([new edition] New York, (Russell and Russell, 1962)

Bentley, Nicolas: *The Victorian scene: a picture book of the period* 1837-1901. (Weidenfeld and Nicolson, 1968)

Bishop, A.S.: *The rise of a central authority for English education.* (Cambridge University Press, 1971)

Birchenough, Charles: *A history of education from* 1800. (University Tutorial Press, 1932)

Blackstone, William: *Commentaries on the laws of England.* 15th edn. (Cadell and Davies, 1809)

Brewis, Elsdon W.: *The history and progress of education.* (Newcastle-upon-Tyne, Cambois colliery, 1881)

Briggs, Harrison, McInnes, Vincent: *Crime and punishment in England: an introductory history.* (University College London Press, 1996)

Cornish, W.R. and Clark, de N.: *Law and society in England* 1750-1950. (Sweet and Maxwell, 1989)

Crowther, M.A.: *The Workhouse system* 1834-1929. (Batsford, 1981)

Emsley, Clive: *Crime and society in England* 1750-1900. (Longmans, 1987)

Fitch, J.G.: *Public education: why is the new Code wanted?* (1861)

Kelly's Trades Directory for Newcastle upon Tyne 1850

Mackenzie, E.: *Descriptive and historical account of Newcastle-upon-Tyne and Gateshead.* (Newcastle, 1827).

Murphy, James: *Church, state and schools in Britain* 1800-1970. (Routledge and Kegan Paul, 1971)

Newcastle Daily Leader [newspaper]

Sanders, Wiley B.: *Juvenile offenders for a thousand years.* (University of North Carolina Press, 1973).

Simon, Brian: *Studies in the history of education* 1780-1870. (Lawrence and Wishart, 1960)

Stephens, W.B.: *Education in Britain* 1750-1914. (Basingstoke, Macmillan, 1998)

Thomas, D.H.: *Reformatory and Industrial Schools: an annotated list* 1854-1933. (Newcastle-upon-Tyne Polytechnic, 1986)

Thomas, D.H.: *The certified Industrial Schools for Catholic boys and girls in the north of England* 1888-1933 (in *Northern Catholic History* no.14 Autumn 1981)

Thomas, D.H.: *The three certified Day Industrial Schools in the north-east of England* (Newcastle City Libraries, 1983)

Thomas, D.H.: *The Newcastle Day Industrial School, and truancy in the* 1880s. (Newcastle City Libraries, 1982)

Thomas, D.H.: *Four Industrial Schools in the north-east of England.* (Durham County Local History Society Bulletin no.26, May 1981)

Times newspaper

Tuckwell, Gertrude: *The state and its children* (1894)

West, E.G.: *Education and the Industrial Revolution.* (Batsford, 1975)

Index